Learning Through Drama in

Learning Through Drama contains drama strategies and lesson plans for use with primary school children both within subject areas and as extended learning opportunities in whole class drama sessions.

This practical handbook explores how to use the greatest resource that teachers have available to them – children's imagination. Play is a natural part of children's lives before they start school, helping them to make sense of their place in the world. Such creativity can be harnessed through drama to enable active and interactive learning experiences throughout the primary years and across the curriculum.

This book will help if:

★ You have never taught drama before but are considering using it in a subject area such as science or history.

★ You are familiar with common drama techniques such as hot seating but would like to try out new approaches.

★ You would like to teach thematic drama units linked to several areas of the curriculum.

★ You would like to find out how drama can be used to inspire speaking, listening and writing.

Includes 36 drama strategies and over 250 cross-curricular activities.

David Farmer is a freelance drama consultant, storyteller, theatre director and author of the best-selling *101 Drama Games and Activities*.

'Even the well-practiced and creative drama teacher will find something in this book that serves as a refresher, reminder or quite simply a new idea... a must-have publication for those serious about the teaching of drama in primary school settings.' - Teaching Drama magazine.

Also by David Farmer:
101 Drama Games and Activities

Learning
through
Drama
in the Primary Years

David Farmer

Illustrations by David Hurtado

www.dramaresource.com
www.learningthroughdrama.com

"I hear and I forget. I see and I remember.
I do and I understand."
- Confucius

This book is dedicated to the two impresarios
who first put me on the stage –
Geoffrey and June Farmer.

About the Author

After training as a primary school teacher, David Farmer worked in theatre-in-education as an actor, writer and director. In 1981 he co-founded *Tiebreak Theatre Company* and was Artistic Director until 2005, producing over 65 acclaimed plays and projects that reached an audience of half a million young people in schools, theatres and festivals. These included commissions by the *Lyric Theatre Hammersmith* and the *Natural History Museum*, sell-out performances at the *Edinburgh Fringe Festival* and tours across Europe, Canada and the USA.

David is now a freelance drama consultant, offering training to educators and arts services to schools. He has mentored projects for *Drama for Learning and Creativity (D4LC)*, *Shakespeare for Schools* and *Creative Partnerships*. He leads storytelling and drama projects with school children and runs courses for teachers, actors, drama practitioners and university students. He is a regular contributor to magazines such as *Teaching Drama* and *Child Education Plus*. He lives in Norwich, Norfolk, (UK) where he runs the website www.dramaresource.com and also teaches yoga.

Contents

Acknowledgements

The author would like to thank Julia Webb for her steadfast support and encouragement throughout the writing of this book – and her eagle eye. Thanks to David Hurtado for bringing the ideas to life through his inspired illustrations and layout design as well as to Kate Llewellin for her helpful suggestions. *Structuring Drama Work: A Handbook of Available Forms in Theatre and Drama* (Neelands and Goode 1990) is a key source for many of the drama strategies.

The author is grateful for permission to reproduce the illustration from *The Gruffalo Pop-Up Theatre Book* (ISBN 978-0230531796), copyright Julia Donaldson and Axel Scheffler, reproduced by permission of Macmillan Children's Books, London, UK.

Using this book

You can dip straight into the main section of this book and try out the drama strategies in any order. The *Introduction* looks at how you can use drama in schools. *Drama Strategies* explores each strategy in detail along with practical examples to use in a variety of contexts. The final section shows you how to draw together the strategies to use in whole class *Drama Lessons*.

INTRODUCTION

★ **Why Use Drama?** explains why drama should be used in education and how it can be used effectively.

★ **Drama and Literacy** explains the unique contribution drama can make to speaking, listening, reading and writing.

★ **Drama Across The Curriculum** gives pointers about using drama in different subject areas.

★ **Getting Started** provides some quick ideas to get you going.

★ **Structuring Drama Activities** gives advice about organising whole class drama lessons or using the strategies across the curriculum.

DRAMA STRATEGIES

★ The main section of the book describes a wide range of activities and approaches to use in drama lessons and across the curriculum.

DRAMA LESSONS

★ This section includes three sample units for different age groups, bringing together the approaches referred to above.

Introduction

This section explores the purpose and impact of using drama in children's learning in and across subject areas. Drama can be used to support and extend literacy – including writing. Advice is given about getting started and structuring drama sessions.

In this section:

- Why Use Drama?

- Whole Class Drama

- Drama and Literacy

- Drama and Writing

- Getting Started

- Structuring Drama

Why Use Drama?

Dramatic activity is already a natural part of most children's lives before they start school in the form of make-believe play, enabling them to make sense of their own identity by exploring meaningful fictional situations that have parallels in the real world. This can be utilised at school through structured play and drama to encourage pupils to learn actively and interactively throughout the primary years and across the curriculum.

Children like to move and to interact with others. In drama we ask them to do exactly this. Rather than sitting still and listening they are encouraged to move, speak and respond to one another. Students who are challenged by reading and writing (including those with English as a second language) often respond more positively to the imaginative and multisensory learning offered by drama. This in turn helps them develop such skills as creativity, enquiry, communication, empathy, self-confidence, cooperation, leadership and negotiation. Most importantly, drama activities are fun – making learning both enjoyable and memorable.

Drama is ideal for cross-curricular learning and is a valuable tool for use in many subject areas. This is explored further in *Drama Across the Curriculum* *(p.5)* and practical examples are given alongside each of the *Drama Strategies* *(p.15)*. In particular, drama develops literacy skills – supporting speaking and listening, extending vocabulary and encouraging pupils to understand and express different points of view. Dramatic activity motivates children to write for a range of purposes.

Drama gives children opportunities to explore, discuss and deal with difficult issues and to express their emotions in a supportive environment. It enables them to explore their own cultural values and those of others, past and present. It encourages them to think and act creatively, thus developing critical thinking and problem-solving skills that can be applied in all areas of learning. Through drama, children are encouraged to take responsible roles and make choices – to participate in and guide their own learning. Teachers can take a more open-ended approach, concentrating on the process of learning at least as much as – if not more than – the product.

Whole Class Drama

Whole class drama (also called *Process Drama*) enables all the students to become involved in an extended drama focussing on learning and enquiry rather than performance – process, not product. Everybody is in role, including the teacher. The approach is child-centred as each pupil's decisions shape the story that unfolds within the drama.

Process drama is experiential – what Gavin Bolton (1979, p.53) calls 'living-through' drama. He describes how participants allow their life experience to inform the drama, enabling them to learn through the process in both a passive and active way:

> *A sense of 'it is happening to me' and 'I am making it happen'.*

Likewise the problems faced and solutions proposed during drama offer the opportunity for children to explore strategies for dealing with situations they may face in the real world.

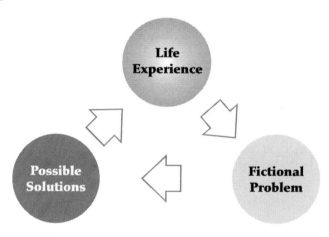

Crucially the children remain aware that they are playing roles, enabling them to reflect on their experiences within the imaginary world. Whole class drama maximises the involvement and enthusiasm of the children. It is common for the drama to sustain interest over a period of several sessions.

Whole class drama can begin with an enquiry question, a problem posed, a story or a topic. The teacher needs to maintain a flexible approach as the outcomes are unknown at the start. The children and teacher may take on a variety of roles to consider the viewpoints of different characters. Afterwards students can reflect on the implications of choices they made for their present lives and their future actions.

There has long been an active debate about the merits of process drama as opposed to performed "product" but this book will help you enjoy the best of both worlds as appropriate to your needs and those of the children. While whole class drama places the emphasis on role-play and living-through, other strategies may also include aspects of performance as part of the learning experience.

Drama strategies can be used as teaching tools for individual subjects and across the curriculum — or to shape a whole class extended drama session. These approaches have grown and developed as a way of making process drama more accessible, drawing on the work of theatre in education companies as well as pioneers such as Brian Way, Dorothy Heathcote, Cecily O'Neill, Gavin Bolton, Jonothan Neelands, Patrice Baldwin and many others.

Drama and Literacy

Drama is a close ally in the development of literacy. Speaking and listening skills are enhanced through drama strategies, role-play and improvisation and by the exchange of opinions and negotiation that naturally occur in group activities. Drama provides the context to improve writing skills, to develop realistic dialogue and to extend vocabulary. Improvisation and storytelling develop children's understanding of narrative structure with a consequent impact on speaking and writing skills.

★ **Group Work:** Discussion encourages students to debate and share ideas, summarise the key points of a story or theme, analyse character behaviour and think about how best to communicate ideas both physically and verbally.

★ **Reading and Listening to Stories:** Drama strategies can be drawn on to deepen the understanding of characters and situations or to explore alternative outcomes. Stories can provide the launch pad for a one-off drama session or several weeks of work.

★ **Language Learning:** Drama is widely used in modern language learning to enable students to develop language skills through *role-play*. Many drama strategies lend themselves to language learning, such as *ten second objects* which can be used to reinforce new vocabulary.

★ **Poetry** has much more to offer than just the recitation of lines. Encourage the children to devise their own performances of poems, acting out narratives or bringing poetic images to life through *still images, tableaux* and *soundscapes*. Use *teacher in role* and *role-play* to deepen and explore issues raised in the poem.

Drama and Writing

Drama can provide children with a meaningful purpose for writing. Pupils become motivated to communicate through emotional identification with characters and their issues. The physical context of drama can particularly inspire boys' writing, especially if they are encouraged to express themselves verbally. You don't need to wait until you get back to the classroom to write. Writing even short phrases and words in the same space as the drama is more immediate than trying to recreate the feelings and ideas back at the desk. Use a variety of writing media such as post-its, clipboards, mini-whiteboards, notebooks, index cards, slips of paper and graffiti sheets.

Writing in role is particularly motivating for children and can cover a range of purposes and audiences – from a diary entry about an event pupils have just "experienced" through improvisation, to letters from WWII evacuees to their mothers or a list of provisions required for an expedition. Children writing in different roles can help to represent varied points of view of the same dramatic situation.

 Tip:

If children are feeling inspired it can be helpful to record what they say in the heat of the moment by scribing it or using audio or video recorders.

Writing in or out of role can include letters, postcards, journals, reportage, interviews, advertisements, poetry, petitions, secret messages, treasure maps, captions, newspaper headlines and so on. Improvised drama is an exciting way of collectively devising a plot that can lead on to the writing of stories, monologues or play scripts. Words and phrases written during drama activities can be compiled into a group poem back in the classroom. Any reflective writing will deepen involvement in the drama and can lead on to further improvisation, artwork and other activities.

Writing done during the session can feed back into the make-believe. Messages can be delivered to characters (children or *teacher in role*) and instructional treasure maps can be tried out. If combining drama with outdoor learning then notes can be left under a stone for the Gruffalo to collect or writing can be done on clipboards to describe fantastic treasures (natural objects) discovered in the woods.

Many of the drama strategies can be used to enhance writing, such as *hot-seating* and *role on the wall* for character development and *still images* for story construction.

Drama Across the Curriculum

Drama strategies can be used as everyday teaching tools for a wide range of subjects. They can illuminate the human dimension of subject areas, such as how scientific progress may impact on individuals and communities. Drama is particularly useful when working on cross-curricular themes as it naturally bridges subject areas. If children take on the roles of archaeologists in Egypt, drama can link history, geography, mythology and art as well as the mathematics of pyramids and the science of building them. Ideas for using drama strategies in individual subject areas are summarised below.

Art

Art can be used as a way of reflecting on drama activity alongside, or as an alternative to, writing and discussion. Drama can help to spark children's creativity and lead them into imaginative and vibrant artwork. Incorporate art into drama by doing collective drawing in groups alongside the drama activities to develop storylines or explore characters and situations.

Geography

Cultural and environmental issues linked to geography can easily be explored through drama. *Teacher in role* and *role on the wall* can be used to present a character from a particular locality and to examine an issue from their perspective. This can lead on to *role-play* with pupils working in pairs or small groups to deepen their understanding. *Still images*, *tableaux* and *soundscapes* can be used to create the atmosphere of different locations and environments.

History

Characters from any historical period can be examined through *hot seating*, *role-play* and *role on the wall*. *Tableaux, improvisation* and *thought tracking* can help to bring historical accounts, illustrations and artwork to life. Key decision-making moments for historical characters can be explored using *conscience alley*.

Mathematics

Maths makes a lot more sense when it is applied to real (or fictional) situations. For younger children, this can be through role-play in shop or restaurant situations. Journeys across the sea, through space or around the world offer potential for acting and storytelling which can include mathematical activities such as calculating journey times and duration, quantities of food and fuel and recording of temperature.

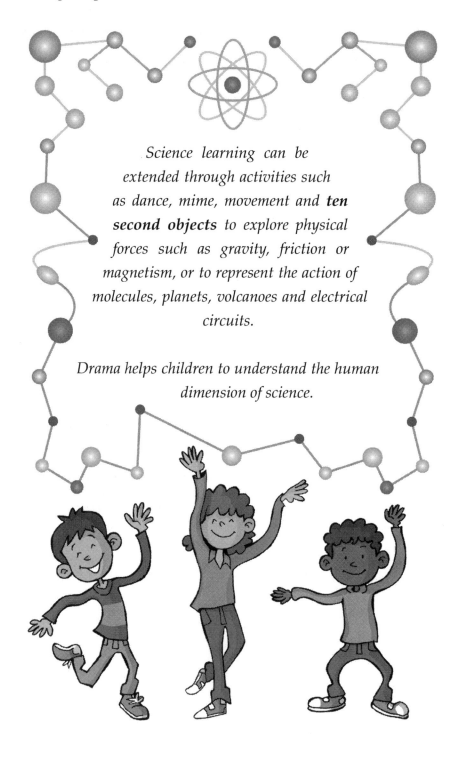

*Science learning can be extended through activities such as dance, mime, movement and **ten second objects** to explore physical forces such as gravity, friction or magnetism, or to represent the action of molecules, planets, volcanoes and electrical circuits.*

Drama helps children to understand the human dimension of science.

Mathematical patterns can be demonstrated and explored through physical movement and dance. Pupils are more likely to remember geometric shapes if they have made them with their own bodies in *ten second objects*. When forming groups, ask pupils to get into even or odd-numbers. Children can even become human bar graphs.

Personal and Social Education

Drama techniques such as *conscience alley* and *image theatre* offer valuable opportunities for pupils to share their opinions and explain their views. *Role-play* and *improvisation* allow them to discover how their behaviour can affect others. Group negotiation and discussion helps to encourage such key skills as listening, working cooperatively and learning to respect one another's similarities and differences.

Science and Technology

Science learning can be extended through activities using dance, mime, movement and *ten second objects* to explore physical forces such as gravity, friction or magnetism, or to represent the action of molecules, planets, geological phenomena or electrical circuits. A journey through the body gives great potential for storytelling and drama. Pupils can model food chains or create human bar graphs to display living representations of scientific results.

The human aspect of science is particularly suitable for exploration through drama. *Where do you stand?* helps to dissect moral dilemmas. *Role play, improvisation* and *teacher in role* can explore how human activity affects living things and the environment, highlighting controversial ethical issues. This can lead on to improvised drama such as the enacting of documentary TV programmes, debates and discussions. Technology can help to extend and develop drama activities through the use of multimedia, such as photography, video, animation and sound recording.

Getting Started

Here are some suggestions that you can introduce as stand-alone teaching strategies or develop as part of a drama lesson. Many more examples are given alongside each of the drama strategies.

★ Begin by trying out one strategy at a time. Select a story or theme and pick a drama strategy that could help to highlight a particular aspect of the topic. Use more techniques as you become familiar with them.

★ Create a *soundscape* of a setting, for example a forest, an urban street or a barren desert and lead on to writing words and phrases suggested by the atmosphere that was created.

★ Choose a colourful character for *hot-seating* or *teacher in role*, such as the Troll in the *Three Billy Goats Gruff* or Ariel in *The Tempest*. Challenge the pupils to see the story from that character's perspective and to come up with alternative endings.

★ If the class is learning about a historical or political event, select a moment where a person is about to make a key decision. Use *conscience alley* to find out what options are available to the character and then reveal the actual decision that was made.

★ Pick out key objects referred to in a story and play *ten second objects* with the pupils before you begin reading. After making the objects, they will enjoy spotting them as they are mentioned in the storytelling.

★ After you have read a story or given an account of an historical event, ask students to select key points of the narrative and to make *still images* for each moment to create your own human storyboard. Dig deeper using *thought tracking*. Bring the scene alive for a few moments through *improvisation*.

★ When you have tried out a few of the strategies in a classroom context, think about progressing to an extended drama session exploring a theme.

Structuring Drama

Use an appropriate space

Drama lessons are often thought of as taking place in a hall or studio but many activities can successfully take place in the classroom. Children can get over-excited when working in a larger space such as a hall and the acoustics can make life difficult. Many interactive pair and small group activities can be carried out at the students' desks. However drama is also about movement and this is an aspect that will motivate many children. If you don't have access to a larger space, then supervise students to clear tables and chairs to the side of the classroom. This can be carried out quickly and safely with practice.

Usually the drama will take place in a neutral empty space. However on occasions you may wish to define a space by using tables, chairs, PE equipment, fabric and other objects to represent specific locations. Melanie Peter (1996) makes creative use of masking tape stuck to walls and floors as a quick method for marking out doors, windows, pathways and so on.

 Tip:

Costumes and Props

Keep an eye out for hats, scarves, saris, tunics, cloaks, glasses, gloves, ribbons, scraps of fabric and a range of interesting objects to spice up your lessons. These can be used by the students or yourself as appropriate.

Begin with clear aims and objectives

As in any teaching, it is essential that you prepare for the drama lesson with clearly focussed aims and objectives. If you just go into the class with a file of drama games and the idea of having fun, chances are you will end up with a lively and out of control group before very long. However, drama games and strategies can be used productively if they are put in the right context. If you are clear about what you are trying to achieve, you can communicate this to the students so that they understand the purpose of the lesson. Outline the session at the beginning and then clarify each activity as you proceed. Use a variety of activities including individual, pair and group work. Include movement-based activities as well as ones based around speaking and listening.

Establish a calm atmosphere with explicit expectations of behaviour

Keeping control in the drama lesson is one of the main reasons why some teachers are reluctant to teach drama. Drama lessons are there to encourage free expression, which explains why many teachers are concerned that this will just lead to noise, over-excitement or even fighting. However with the right approach any teacher can lead a focussed drama lesson where pupils learn to express themselves positively, develop teamwork and many other skills.

Pupils need to be clear about your expectations of acceptable and unacceptable behaviour during drama activities. It helps if you establish a clear routine from the start. If pupils are coming into a designated space for drama such as the hall or studio, then make it clear how they should behave from the beginning, for example sitting quietly in a circle.

 Tip:

Freeze/Go

This game encourages awareness of moving around safely as a member of a group in the space and introduces a control signal that will quickly get students' attention. Ask everyone to spread out around the space. Explain that when you give the signal "Go", pupils should start walking around the room. When you say "Freeze", they should stop and freeze every muscle. Try this out and look for accurate and quick responses. Encourage children to change direction every now and again, rather than walk in a circle or with their friends. Experiment with moving faster or slower. Now, when you need to quickly get attention during a lively activity, you can just call "Freeze!"

As a fun challenge, you can extend the activity by explaining that the instructions are now reversed: when you say "Freeze" you mean "Go" and when you say "Go" you mean "Freeze"! See how many children you can catch out in this way.

The drama strategies outlined in this book are carefully structured to enable students to focus their creativity and energy in a controlled manner. Some activities will naturally lead to increased noise levels, but as long as the students are focussed and productive – and you are not disturbing others – then accept this as a natural part of proceedings. You just need to make sure you have established a clear "Stop" signal such as raising one arm in the air, which should be followed as quickly as possible by all the students quietly stopping what they are doing, facing you and raising an arm as well. Using the "Freeze!' signal referred to above is very effective.

A musical instrument such as a tambourine or small bell can be useful for noisier activities.

Consult students about acceptable guidelines

You can develop students' motivation and commitment to activities by involving them in establishing clear rules. Ask them what they think would help the sessions to run smoothly. Develop some guidelines that can be edited with the group's consensus into a code of conduct or drama contract to be displayed in the space. Then when you point out inappropriate behaviour you can refer to the rule that students have agreed to.

Give clear explanations and cues to keep the students on task

When introducing activities explain the steps involved clearly before giving pupils the signal to start. There is nothing worse than beginning by saying, "I want you to work with a partner…" You will lose students' attention immediately as they focus on who they want to work with. Explain first what you want to achieve through the activity, how they will be expected to do this and how much time they should take. It may be helpful to model the activity on your own or with a student partner. Tell them whether they will be working on their own, with a partner or in a group and finally give them the signal to begin.

Group work

Drama provides a valuable opportunity for pupils to work in groups. As well as benefitting from sharing ideas, they will learn more about leadership, negotiation and cooperation. As students listen to different views, it is essential that they are encouraged to respect one another's opinions. Give them time to discuss their ideas but encourage them to move on quickly to trying things out. Working physically gives students the chance to experiment and often brings new possibilities that would not have appeared through discussion alone.

During activities move from group to group to help pupils negotiate with one another. Ensure that you are enabling them to come up with ideas rather than leading too prescriptively. Your role is to help them clarify ideas, to challenge and extend their thinking – while giving them the space to gel as a group.

Encourage students to respect one another's work

As drama involves so much creativity, students will enjoy and benefit from watching each other's work, whether it is a rehearsed scene or work in progress. Students also need to develop good audience skills. While groups are waiting to show their own work, they probably want to continue discussing and developing their ideas instead of watching and listening to the other groups. One way around this is to encourage them to make positive comments about each other's presentations. When the first group is in place, nominate another group whose task it will be to feedback on the performance. When the first group has finished showing the work, ask for three positive comments from the nominated group. In this way groups will be encouraged to watch one another, to give supportive comments and to notice what could be done to improve their own work.

Evaluate through discussion and more activity

Allow time for students to plan and reflect on what they have done. This can happen at any time during the session. Out-of-role discussion helps students to crystallise what they most enjoyed and what they are learning from the activities. Sitting in a circle is a tried and tested way of recognising that the group has a shared purpose and that everybody has an equal voice. Many drama activities themselves can be used for evaluation, such as *conscience alley, essence machines, rumours, thought tracking, still images* and *where do you stand?* Having a camera or video recorder to hand helps students to recall and evaluate work, as does reflection through art and writing *(p.4).* Of course make sure you evaluate the session yourself to discover what you might want to change or develop next time.

Drama Strategies

Drama strategies (also known as *drama techniques* and *drama conventions*) are the everyday tools of the drama teacher. They have been developed for a wide range of purposes and are drawn from such diverse sources as drama practitioners, theatre directors and theatre in education (TIE) companies. They help to develop children's enquiry skills, fostering communication, negotiation, understanding and creativity. Drama strategies can enhance performance skills including storytelling, character development, mime and movement.

There is no right or wrong way of using drama strategies. As you become more familiar with them, their appropriateness for different situations will become clearer. You can use them in any order; you can adapt them, mix them together and before too long will find that you are devising new approaches yourself to add to this collection. These techniques can be easily adapted to suit a wide range of age groups, learning styles and curricular needs.

What follows is a selection of effective and flexible approaches suitable for use in a wide range of situations. They are grouped according to their application although the categories are not mutually exclusive. Practical examples are given alongside each strategy to show how they may be used within subject areas or across the curriculum. To get you started, shown opposite are eight of my favourite strategies that can be used again and again to actively involve children in their own learning

Key: R 1 2

*The symbols are used to recommend activities for **Reception** (4-5 years), **Key Stage 1** (5-7 years) and **Key Stage 2** (7-11 years).*

A suggested duration is given above each drama strategy. This is for guidance and allowances should be made for different groups.

Role Play Strategies

Role play enables students to explore contrasting viewpoints, step into the past or future and travel to any location in their imagination. The teacher can actively participate in the dramatic process, making it possible to present challenging points of view and to stimulate thought, discussion and action by pupils.

In this section:

- Role Play

- Teacher in Role

- Mantle of the Expert

- Hot Seating

- Thought Tracking

- Role On The Wall

- Meetings

- Rumours

- Telephone Conversations

Role Play

   Pairs, Groups, Whole Class 15 minutes +

> The student takes on the role of a character to explore an alternative point of view.

Why use it?

The ability to step into another character's shoes through make-believe play comes naturally to most children. This can be used to great effect in drama, challenging pupils to develop a more sensitive understanding of contrasting viewpoints. By adopting a role, students can step into the past or future and travel to any location, dealing with issues on emotional, moral and intellectual levels. They can play familiar and unfamiliar roles in known or unknown settings. They can grapple with problems, deal with success and failure in the knowledge that it is only make-believe.

The ability of children to explore ideas through role-play and learn through communication with one another is used widely at foundation stage in role-play areas and can be used effectively throughout the primary years and beyond to illuminate subjects across the curriculum.

How do you do it?

When setting up role-play it is important that children are "contracted in". This simply means that they should be clear when the make-believe begins and ends so that even though they become immersed in their roles, they know that the situation is not real. This enables them to be objective about the process so that they can talk about what happened whilst they were 'pretending to be someone else' and learn from their experiences. They need to comprehend what happened during the shared fiction so that they can understand implications for their behaviour in the real world. This is equally important when working as *teacher in role*.

Variations

Role-play is an essential part of most drama activities and usually takes place in the following formats or a combination of them. Students in role can interact with *teacher in role* in any of these categories.

Individuals

Individual role play includes occupational mime activities where children carry out jobs and activities in role such as the animals helping *Farmer Duck* (Waddell 1991), detectives examining clues, archaeologists unearthing a find, owners looking after pets or explorers cataloguing new specimens.

Pairs

Two students take on roles in the same situation and improvise or prepare a piece of drama, such as Red Riding Hood and Grandma, a spaceman and an alien, an environmental campaigner and a factory owner.

Groups

Once pupils are able to work together cooperatively they can progress to small group work. They may need advice about how to organise themselves. Although they need to spend time in preparatory discussion they should be encouraged to move onto practical work as soon as possible.

Whole Class

It is easy to move from individual into whole class role-play. The roles can be generic, for example market traders, townspeople or woodland animals. This means that children are not singled out and they can support each other through talk and interaction. *Teacher in role* makes it easy to put pupils into role, for example the teacher can be the overseer of a workhouse with the children in role as inmates, or a villager discussing what to do about the *Iron Man* (Hughes 1968).

Collective Role

A single character can be jointly played by members of a group so that any one of them may speak as that person. This ensures that less confident students benefit from the support of the group without being singled out. When asked a question any student may take a turn to answer as the character. This can be done sitting in a circle with consecutive turn-taking or with random answers from a group. See *Listen To Me (p.137)* for an example of collective role.

Collective role is an effective way of exploring complex characters which may be too challenging for individuals. The strategy allows many students to experience role-play at the same time and makes the most of shared knowledge and understanding. It is even possible to have more than one group involved so that different collective characters can speak to each other.

Another variation on collective role is known as *Voices in the Head*. A group of students represents one character's thoughts like a Greek chorus. Members of the group whisper the character's thoughts to one student who acts as the mouthpiece, choosing which thoughts to speak. Younger pupils often work in this way quite naturally – for example when one of them is telling a story or explaining something, others will whisper suggestions to them if they get stuck.

Teacher in Role   2

      Whole Class | 15 minutes +

> The teacher (or other adult) assumes the role of a character to guide and develop students' learning.

Why use it?

The teacher is able to directly participate in the dramatic process and influence it from the inside. This makes it possible to present challenging and controversial points of view and to stimulate thought, discussion and action by pupils. Teacher in role validates and supports the children's involvement in a make-believe situation by enabling the teacher to work and 'play' alongside them. It is an instant way of setting a scene and directly involving the pupils. Children are used to stepping into and out of role in everyday play and are likely to be keen to participate.

How do you do it?

Teacher in role does not require great acting skills. It can be seen as an extension of the ever-changing role-play that we all experience – whether as parent, child, teacher, student, colleague and so on. The strategy simply involves 'stepping into somebody else's shoes' for a while to put forward their point of view. This can be done by subtly changing your tone of voice and body language to communicate key attitudes, emotions and viewpoints. If you can use different voices for characters when you tell a story then you are certainly able to carry out teacher in role.

It won't take much for most children to believe in your character although the use of a token prop or piece of costume will clarify when you are stepping in and out of role: *"When I put on this scarf I will be Anne Frank"*, or *"When I sit in this chair I will be the King"*. Although not essential, you may wish to place furniture and props to represent a different place – but keep it simple.

If you are unsure how to begin try *hot-seating* first. This will give you valuable experience of assuming a role in relation to the students and responding to their comments and questions. Hot-seating becomes teacher in role when you start to take the lead in the discussion or when you encourage pupils to participate as you bring movement to the character. This can be as simple as walking around and engaging with individual students or involving them in *occupational mime* activities to deepen their belief.

In her analysis of Dorothy Heathcote's approach, Wagner (1976) discusses how teacher in role completely alters the relationship between teacher and pupils:

> *When the teacher is in role as a participant in the drama, there is no reason for the students to show undue respect or deference. This, for most teachers, is a new stance, one which allows for a real exchange to take place easily and spontaneously.*

You may choose to play a high-status character, an equal, or a subordinate role – whatever is useful in developing the drama.

High status

An authoritative role such as an official or other commanding character enables you to remain in control and give clear guidance. While this may seem like an attractive option it can be perceived as too similar to your teaching role and may be inhibiting for the pupils, affecting their willingness to contribute.

Equal status

An equal role enables you to be 'one of them' – a fellow villager, jury member, explorer and so on. You are in the same predicament as the children but can guide by asking questions.

Low status

You can still maintain the focus of the class by playing a low-status role – someone in need of help or guidance. Students are likely to be sympathetic to such a character as it puts them in an 'expert' role.

 Tip:

> *Costume Ideas:*
>
> *Hats, crowns, scarves, aprons, bags, cloaks, shawls, dressing gowns, jackets, walking sticks and umbrellas can be useful character signifiers – and you don't need full costume. It should be something you can put on and take off easily.*

To begin with, try asking questions of pupils, putting them into role as members of a specific group and encouraging them to question you in return. It helps if you reply to their questions or comments as though they are already in role.

You can engage the attention of the class at an early stage by not announcing who you are and encouraging them to find out. By speaking in character about your situation you can give students clues to involve them in the story. Your character will soon gain the children's interest by seeking their help with some kind of predicament:

> *I can see that we have a lot of work to do. If our patients are going to survive then we shall have to wash down all the floors and walls. We can't just leave bandages on the floor – they need to be cleared up. I know that you nurses have been working under considerable pressure but we will have even more patients arriving soon from the Crimean front. Can you help me to make everything spick and span before they arrive?*

If the pupils have not worked out who you are by now then you can give them more obvious pointers:

*My mother said to me before I left, "Do you really know what you're
letting yourself in for, Florence?"*

In role you can ask how to do something or what something is as an
engaging way of checking students' understanding and encouraging them
to use explanatory language. The deeper involvement of pupils brought
about by teacher in role naturally opens the door to other drama strategies
such as *improvisation* as well as leading on to art, writing and other forms
of expression and interpretation. You can lead into cross-curricular activity
– for example asking directions can lead to map-making.

Don't be afraid to play somebody of the opposite gender or a fantasy
character. You are not limited to portraying human characters – anything is
fair game, ranging from animals discussing what it's like to be part of a food
chain to legendary monsters such as the 'poor misunderstood' Minotaur.
Most importantly teacher in role is not all about the teacher playing a part;
it's about providing challenges and stimuli to actively involve children in
learning experiences. Remember that you are portraying an attitude rather
than attempting to give an Oscar-winning performance.

You can present contrasting views during a drama session by playing
more than one character – as long as you make it clear who you are each
time. Involving teaching assistants and other adults opens up even more
possibilities as well as giving you moral support. When you have stepped
out of role take time to discuss any issues raised to ensure the pupils make
a connection between the fictional drama and the real world.

A natural development of teacher in role is *mantle of the expert*, which is
described in the next section.

Examples

Art/History

★   Take the role of a character in a painting or photograph that the children
    have been studying. Explain that you will be one of the people in the
    picture and the students need to work out who you are by asking
    questions. You can start off and finish in the pose of the person in the
    picture.

Geography

★   Candidates for teacher in role include explorers, aid workers, eco-
    tourists, people from other cultures, people whose decisions affect

land development or whose livelihoods are affected by geographic phenomena or change.

History

★ Liven up any history lesson by taking the role of characters using hot-seating and teacher in role. Even five minutes of this technique will stick in children's minds. You needn't choose a famous person – you can play a bystander at an event. With more experience you will be able to use the approach alongside other strategies to involve your class in a developed drama lesson.

★ Characters might include: a Roman centurion, an Ancient Egyptian child, a workhouse overseer, an archaeologist, Boudicca, Yuri Gagarin, a member of parliament, a Saxon farmer and so on.

Literacy

★ Stories are the greatest source of characters – ranging from the Gruffalo to the Minotaur, from Red Riding Hood to Oliver Twist, from Anansi to Cyclops; great fun and learning can be had from bringing literary characters to life. Use the characters to recap on the story, to view it from a different vantage point or to give it a new ending.

Science

★ An excited inventor explains a new invention for the first time.

★ An opinionated farmer explains why genetic engineering is a good idea. Make sure you leave space for the children's responses!

★ A television weather reporter explains her job.

Mantle of the Expert   3

| R 1 2 | Whole Class | 45 minutes + |

> The creation of a fictional world where students assume the roles of
> experts in a designated field.

Why use it?

Mantle of the Expert[1] (MoE) is based on the premise that treating children
as responsible experts increases their engagement and confidence. They
can perceive a real purpose for learning and discovering together in an
interactive and proactive way – gathering skills and knowledge they
can apply to their everyday lives. MoE encourages creativity, improves
teamwork, communication skills, critical thought and decision-making.
While the focus is on the enquiry process, it can often lead to real outcomes
such as writing letters, printing leaflets or designing products.

Being treated as experts empowers pupils to actively explore issues across
the curriculum, assume responsible roles, solve problems and make
decisions in guiding the process and its outcomes. The technique can be
used as a stand-alone activity within a drama session but is most effective
when used over an extended period of time as children's engagement
becomes heightened so that they are keen to learn more. The children's
imaginary roles can take them into real or fictional places ranging from
ancient Rome to fabled lands and outer space.

How do you do it?

A problem or task is established and the pupils are contracted-in or 'framed'
as an enterprise or business – a team of experts using imaginative role-
play to explore the issue. Usually an imaginary client such as a museum

---

[1] The approach was devised and developed by British drama in education expert Dorothy
Heathcote from the 1960's onwards.

commissions the class – for example as a team of archaeologists to excavate a newly discovered tomb in Egypt. It is possible to link the project with real organisations which can write to the students, invite them to visit or even send representatives in role to the classroom. However this is not essential as the teaching staff can play many different roles.

The teacher's task is to guide the drama, stepping in and out of role as necessary, providing encouragement and motivation to the experts. It can be helpful to draft in classroom assistants or other adults to play additional roles from time to time to heighten pupil engagement. Students assume roles within the imaginary community and their involvement may take the form of almost any learning approach, ranging from improvisation and occupational mime to reading, writing, designing, making, research and discussion. The projects undertaken are not limited to one subject area. They are naturally cross-curricular, often involving literacy and maths as well as other disciplines such as science, history, geography, art and ICT.

It is not possible to do *Mantle of the Expert* full justice in this book. It is well worth visiting the dedicated website[2] which provides information, training courses and in-depth lesson plans. Topics covered include theme park design, a mountain rescue, living museums, Tutankhamen's tomb and the Fire of London. Below are a few outlines of the types of projects that can be done.

Examples

Cross-Curricular

★ The children are concerned about global warming. Using role-play and internet research they investigate the impact of drought on an African village. Framed as expert scientists they help to design more effective wells. As an ad-agency they explore ways to raise awareness and fund-raise in their own school.

★ The enterprise is a local newspaper office gathering local and world news for publication in a weekly edition. Children are involved as editors, sub-editors, journalists, photographers, researchers, cartoonists, designers, printers and so on. They research using the internet, telephone calls and interviews in the local area.

★ A manufacturing company is commissioning a new range of environmentally friendly products which must be designed, packaged and marketed.

---

[2] www.mantleoftheexpert.com

★ The pupils are framed as librarians campaigning to encourage families to read. They organise events, write and tell stories, design and distribute posters.

★ The enterprise is a Hollywood movie company making the true story of Christopher Columbus' 'discovery' of America.

★ Astronomers and astronauts launch the first manned mission to another planet.

In the UK, many schools have found Mantle of the Expert to be a highly effective strategy and have adopted it as a whole-school cross-curricular approach:

> *"(Mantle of the Expert) creates such a rich fictional context for learning and it uses the richest of all our resources – the children's imagination... It builds on children's natural ability to imagine worlds and to role play and they slip easily in and out of the dramatic situations explored."*
>
> *- Jenny Burrell, Teacher, Norwich. (Burrell 2007)*

See also: *Meetings, Role Play, Teacher in Role.*

Hot Seating

  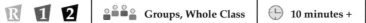 Groups, Whole Class | 10 minutes +

The student or teacher answers questions in role about the background, behaviour and motivation of a character.

Why use it?

Hot seating may be used for exploring the motivations of any real or fictitious character. The method can easily be used across the curriculum, ranging from history and geography through to personal and social development. This strategy helps to develop questioning skills within the rest of the group. Hot seating can also be used to help actors develop confidence in their character roles during rehearsals.

How do you do it?

The traditional approach is for the person playing the character to sit on a chair in front of the group. Pupils are then invited to ask questions. These can begin with simple facts, such as name, age and occupation and move on to more personal areas. If a student is being hot-seated it is helpful if the teacher takes on the role of facilitator to guide the questioning in constructive directions.

To help students begin you can try hot-seating children in pairs (e.g. a pair of street urchins) or in groups (e.g. environmental protesters, refugees). If the background of the character is familiar to the pupils, then it may not be necessary for those playing the characters to do much preparation. Although some roles obviously require research you may be surprised at how much detail students can add from their own imaginations. It is important that the rest of the group are primed to ask pertinent questions. Don't get bogged down in facts during hot seating, but concentrate on personal feelings and observations instead.

To add a touch of fun you can enlist the help of a teaching assistant or a confident child to play the role of a chat show host who introduces the character to the class and helps to field the questions. If a character isn't fully revealing the truth to the group, *thought tracking* can be used to find out what the character may really be thinking.

Hot seating can be used in the middle of an *improvisation* by freezing the improvisation and interviewing individual characters. It can be helpful in rehearsals for actors who have become too attached to the script, enabling them to forget their concerns about learning lines and to explore the background and motivations of a character instead. *Role on the wall* is effective for developing characters and can be used alongside hot seating. You can hot seat more than one character at a time to explore different viewpoints.

Examples

In the following examples either the teacher or the students can be hot seated depending on their level of knowledge about the characters. The more experience of the technique the children gain, the better they will become.

History

★ Characters to hot seat include famous people such as Florence Nightingale, President Kennedy or Tutankhamen as well as ordinary people like a chimney sweep, a Roman soldier or a Saxon farmer. Students can be asked to research historical characters with opposing points of view and then be hot-seated by the class as part of a debate.

Literacy

★ Characters from a story can be hot seated to give different points of view – for example, Red Riding Hood, the Wolf and Grandma or the Billy Goats Gruff and the Troll. Ask the children which characters they would like to meet from the story. You may also introduce peripheral characters or even ones that don't appear such as relatives of one of the main characters.

Personal and Social Education

★ Following a group improvisation about a bullying incident the bully, the witnesses and the bully's friends can be hot seated (together or separately) to explore their feelings about what they did and whether they can learn to behave differently.

See also: *Role on the Wall, Role Play, Teacher in Role, Thought Tracking.*

Thought Tracking 5

    Pairs, Groups, Whole Class   5 minutes

Students speak aloud the thoughts of their character in a still image.

Why use it?

Thought tracking (also called *thought tapping*) is a quick-fire strategy enabling children to verbally express their understanding of characters and situations without the need for rehearsal. Students gain confidence to speak in front of others, preparing the ground for them to move into extended *improvisation*. It is surprisingly easy for pupils to identify with a role and express their thoughts after holding a still image for a few moments. The teacher can efficiently gather feedback from all the students.

How do you do it?

Thought tracking is a natural follow-up to *still images* and *freeze frames*. Once children have made an image, explain that when you tap them on the shoulder you would like them to speak the thoughts or feelings of their character aloud. At the beginning this may just be one or two words but children will soon gain confidence to express themselves in longer sentences. It doesn't take long to thought-track each child in a group so that you reveal a wide range of attitudes and feelings from different characters.

Instead of tapping pupils on the shoulder you can just point to or look at them. Another variation is to hold a cardboard thought-bubble or speech-bubble above their head. Some pupils may find this visual cue helpful and it can be used to reveal the difference between what a character is saying and thinking. After practice many pupils will be able to speak their in-role thoughts without being told when to speak.

Students may want to be inanimate objects or animals in a still image. This is fine, as animal characters can have thoughts – such as "grrrr" or "I'm hungry" and you may find that even a lamppost can express its opinion,

"What can you see at the top of the beanstalk?"

especially if you have used *speaking objects* with pupils. You can ask characters specific questions such as what they feel about another character, what they are dreaming or what they want to do next. Thought tracking can easily be employed in the classroom with children at their desks.

Thought tracking can be used to slow down the action or add extra detail during a group improvisation. This is done by freezing the action in the scene and then tapping characters on the shoulder. The strategy can also be used as a stepping-stone to lead from still images into improvisation *(p.96)*.

★　If a child is nervous or unsure what to say, just ask other students for suggestions – usually there will be no shortage of ideas.

★　Children can write down what they say during thought tracking and draw pictures, storyboards or comic-strips with the comments added in speech and thought bubbles.

★　Thought tracking can be used across the curriculum with all the suggested activities outlined in the section on *still images (p.63)*.

Alter Ego

Alter Ego is a variation on thought tracking. Pupils work in pairs. One student enacts a role while the other positions him or herself nearby and speaks aloud what the character may actually be thinking. The performer needs to allow time for the thoughts to be spoken. You could try alter-egos for Red Riding Hood and the Wolf when they first meet, or for older pupils an improvised chat show hosting a debate between politicians while the alter egos reveal what they really think.

 Tip:

Prompts

Useful sentence beginnings for children to use in thought tracking include:
I can see, hear, feel, smell, taste…   I hope…
I wish…   I feel…
I wonder…   I imagine…

See also: *Conscience Alley, Hot Seating, Role Play, Speaking Objects, Still Images.*

Role on the Wall

 6

| **1** **2** | **Pairs, Groups, Whole Class** | **15 minutes +** |

A collaborative way of generating information and ideas about a character through written contributions to a drawing.

Why use it?

Role on the wall enables students to pool their ideas and develop understanding of a character, whether real or fictional.

How do you do it?

A large or life-size outline of a body (this can be as simple as a gingerbread man) is drawn on a sheet of paper, which can later be displayed on the wall. This is often done by carefully drawing around one of the participants lying on the sheet of paper. Alternatively you can project an image onto the paper and draw around the silhouette.

Words or phrases describing the character are written directly onto the drawing by the teacher and pupils or attached with sticky notes. You can include *known facts* such as physical appearance, age, family, location and occupation as well as *subjective ideas* such as personality, likes/dislikes, friends/enemies, attitudes, motivations, secrets and dreams.

There are many ways of organising the written comments. Here are a few:

★ Known facts can be written around the silhouette and thoughts and feelings inside.

★ Comments made by other characters are jotted down around the outline and the character's own thoughts on the inside.

★ Write what is known about the character inside the outline and questions that students want to ask around the outside.

★ Use different parts of the body for different subjects, e.g. thoughts and ideas in the head, feelings in the heart, known facts in the arms and legs.

★ Key lines spoken by the character can be added. These may be lines from a play or book, or quotes by real people such as historical or scientific figures.

★ The comments can be organised easily using sticky notes and coloured pens.

The class can return to add information and ideas as they learn more about the character over time. The strategy works well in combination with other approaches such as *hot seating*. Once pupils are familiar with the process you can develop several roles at once. Lay out large sheets of paper and students can work on them in groups, swopping round after a while to read and add to other groups' work.

To flesh out the details students can develop backgrounds for the characters through improvisation and role-play. Role on the wall can also be used to help actors understand more about the character they are playing.

Examples

History

★ Historical character: Show what he or she achieved on the inside with dates, important events and names or pictures of related people on the outside.

Literacy

★ Use the strategy to create characters for a play or story or to examine any existing character.

★ Small groups can create role on the wall diagrams for different characters from the same story. Display them together so that their attitudes toward one another can be compared.

Science

★ Famous scientist: Place descriptions or drawings of inventions and discoveries on the inside of the drawing and contemporary influences or events on the outside.

See also: *Hot-seating, Improvisation, Role Play, Sculpting, Thought Tracking.*

Meetings 7

| **1** **2** | 👥 Whole Class | 🕐 15 minutes + |

> An improvised gathering held in role to discuss views about a problem and how it can be resolved.

Why use it?

Meetings provide a way of debating big subjects and seeing issues from different viewpoints. They enable students to present, appreciate and interpret different points of view while maintaining a role over a period of time. Meetings provide a focal point for delivering information, planning a strategy, exploring ideas or discussing a problem during an extended *whole class drama* session or when using *mantle of the expert*. The strategy provides a formal structure for working as *teacher in role* and can be used to bring together characters from a story or play.

How do you do it?

Everybody should be in role including the teacher, who may assume leadership. The group can be gathered in a circle or in rows, depending on the type of meeting. Children can be in *collective role (p.18)* or take on roles of individual characters. They may be divided into smaller groups to represent different factions such as workers, villagers and demonstrators. It may help to use *rituals* using sounds or objects to start the meeting, to call for attention or to indicate turn taking. The meeting could take place in a village hall or it might be a street rally, a union meeting, a staff meeting, a court trial and so forth.

Examples

Geography:

★ Students meet in role as parents, business-owners and car-drivers to discuss how best to make the roads safe outside the school.

★ A public meeting to discuss the damming of a river as part of the construction of a hydroelectric power station. Students in role as residents, power company staff and protestors.

History:

★ The villagers of Eyam meet to discuss the threat of the Black Death.

★ An infamous historical character is put on trial. The children are allocated roles including jury members, witnesses, prosecution and defence counsels and judge.

★ A billeting officer holds a meeting to ask villagers to house evacuee children and to discuss their concerns.

Literacy

★ In *The Pied Piper of Hamelin* (Browning) the townspeople meet to discuss what to do about the rats.

★ In *Frog in Winter* (Velthuijs 1994) Frog's friends meet to discuss how they can cheer him up.

★ In *Farmer Duck* (Waddell 1991) the animals meet to see how they can help the over-worked duck.

★ In *Romeo and Juliet* the Capulets have a meeting to decide what to do about the Montagues (and vice-versa).

Science:

★ Insects from a compost heap meet to decide how to share out the things they like to eat.

★ A hive of bees meets with a swarm of butterflies to discuss what they can do about the dwindling wild flower population.

★ Use the format of a live TV chat show to frame a debate about a science issue such as climate change or genetic engineering. The class are the audience, you (or a student) are the presenter. Individual pupils represent contrasting views on the panel with a roving "microphone" picking up audience questions and comments.

See also: *Mantle of the Expert, Ritual, Role Play, Teacher in Role.*

Rumours

1 **2** | Whole Class | 5 minutes +

> Improvised comments are passed amongst students to generate and spread ideas about characters or situations.

Why use it?

Everybody loves a rumour. The intriguing thing about them is that they don't have to be true. Rumours enable us to take a story and expand it sideways. Pupils can guess about characters' motives and in the process summarise their progress and generate new ideas. This strategy provides a refreshing alternative to teacher-led discussion, giving pupils the opportunity to communicate their understanding in a playful way. It enables students to progress from pair or group work to sharing ideas more widely. Rumours can be seen as a miniaturised form of storytelling and help to develop speaking and listening skills.

How do you do it?

There are no rumours without a story, whether it is one told to the students or one they have improvised. As gossip-mongers they will need a role, either as a 'neutral' bystander or a story character, which will influence the kind of rumours they spread and how true they are. The activity itself needs just long enough for each student to move around the space to mingle and gossip to a few others. When pupils change partners they can pass on their own rumours or ones they have heard previously – which of course they may choose to modify or exaggerate. In this way a complex collective story can soon be developed.

The conspiratorial nature of rumours means that students may enjoy the concept of keeping ideas secret from the teacher. You can capitalise on this by suggesting that pupils whisper the rumours to one another. You will also need a way of gathering students' ideas – perhaps through *improvisation,* an in-role *meeting,* writing or discussion. You can use the strategy to illustrate how stories are generated, why facts easily become confused and why some rumours spread more widely.

Teacher in role can start off a rumour – or a few contrasting ones – which the students speculate about (see examples below). If the children are in character and involved in the story then they may already be sufficiently motivated and engaged to come up with rumours themselves. If they need guidance then you could have some suggestions written on slips of paper as a back up.

★ Rumours are great for exploring different opinions about a character: *"Did you know that Jack has bought his mother a new house?" "Actually I heard that he is very greedy and can't wait to get back to the Giant's Castle."*

★ In a *whole class drama* rumours can be used to spread information and stories between groups, for example Robin Hood's Outlaws and the people of Nottingham.

★ Secretly nominate some pupils as spies who are trying to find out what is going on in a situation. Who do the others think they can trust?

★ Rumours work well for formulating a secret plan such as escaping from a workhouse, breaking out of prison or organising a spying mission.

Examples

Two examples given together indicate contradictory rumours which could be spread by the teacher or characters. Of course you should encourage the pupils to come up with their own rumours too.

Geography

★ (a) *"I've heard that a new factory is going to be built near the village. There could be some new jobs going."* (b) *"Have you heard about that new factory? All the lorries are going to drive right through the village centre."*

History

★ (a)*"I saw some long ships with tall striped sails on the horizon. Shall we organise a welcoming committee?"* (b) *"Have you seen those war ships? We'd better defend the town."*

★ *"Someone told me that if you sign up for Nelson's Navy you get as much food as you can eat three times a day – and your own cabin!"*

Literacy

★ Ask children to choose a character from a story. As they walk around they should whisper rumours from that character's point of view, for example *"I'm sure somebody has been eating my porridge"* or *"Cinderella is really lazy. She's not as pretty as me."*

★ Stop a story halfway through and encourage the children to gossip about the characters and what they have been up to: *"Have you seen that strange fluffy duckling? I'm sure he doesn't belong here. He doesn't look quite right."*

★ (a) *"The grass looks much greener on the other side of the river."* (b) *"I've heard there's something big and dangerous living under the bridge."*

★ *"The sky is falling!"*

Personal and Social Education

★ Rumours can be used to look at how verbal bullying can take place – see *Listen to Me (p.135).*

See also: *Storytelling, Telephone Conversations.*

Telephone Conversations

   | Pairs, Groups, Whole Class | 5 minutes +

Pupils speak in role as if having a conversation on the telephone.

Why use it?

Children naturally mime phone conversations when playing and we can use this in drama to represent and explore different viewpoints. Conversations can be one-sided between a student and an imaginary character or among two or more pupils. The activity enables children to focus on the content of what is said without having to worry about how their character should physically behave.

Telephone conversations can also be used by the teacher to "phone" individual pupils or to "receive information" to move the action forward. Telephone conversations can be recorded to listen to or transcribe later.

How do you do it?

The strategy can be used at any point where characters need to converse or solve a problem. There is no need to use an actual prop to represent the phone – it is easy to simply mime the handset. If the conversations are one-sided then all the students can participate simultaneously, otherwise students can be divided into pairs or groups.

Examples

Geography

★ The teacher in role as an injured miner phones the rescue crew who have to decide how to reach the casualty and what equipment to bring.

★ Pairs improvise a conversation with a pen pal in another country.

★ Mission Control calls the first astronaut to set foot on Mars.

History

★ In a ***whole-class drama*** students "travel back in time" and then call the teacher with individual updates of their observations, for example journalists phone in live reports from the Battle of Hastings.

★ As a variation on ***hot-seating***, the teacher or a student plays a character from history while class members phone in their questions.

Literacy

★ In pairs, one child advises Gerald how he can feel better about himself in *Giraffes Can't Dance* (Andreae 2001).

★ *Horrid Henry*'s mother or Hermione Grainger (from *Harry Potter*) phones an agony aunt asking for advice.

★ Two story characters gossip about another character on the telephone.

Speaking and Listening

★ Giving and receiving good or bad news.

★ Students in role play a parent explaining to a teacher why her child is late for school.

See also: *Role Play, Rumours, Teacher in Role.*

Storytelling Strategies

Storytelling is one of the simplest and perhaps most compelling forms of dramatic and imaginative activity. Narration can be used by the teacher to create atmosphere and to move the drama on. Pupils develop their storytelling skills through drama and this can help to improve their writing, speaking and listening.

In this section:

- Storytelling

- Narration (by the teacher)

- Narration (by the students)

- Visualisation

- Guided Tour

- One Word At A Time

- Bags And Boxes

Storytelling

Pairs, Groups, Whole Class | 10 minutes +

Storytelling is one of the simplest and perhaps most compelling forms of dramatic and imaginative activity.

Why use it?

Listening to, telling and re-telling stories enables children to make more sense of the world around them, to share experiences with one another and to develop their imagination and creativity. Storytelling helps to improve pupils' speaking and listening skills and to increase motivation for reading and written work. Being able to tell a story orally is the first step towards writing it. Storytelling encourages pupils to see events from different perspectives. With the bedtime story fast becoming an endangered species, schools are well-placed to encourage children to tell stories in the hope that their enthusiasm will rub off on their parents.

How do you do it?

Storytelling can be used as a stand-alone activity or combined with other drama strategies. A good place to start is by telling stories to your pupils and encouraging them to share stories with one another. All of us can become engaging storytellers with a little practice. There may also be members of staff who are particularly skilled at telling stories, or you could invite a professional storyteller into the school. Listen to each other, watch

 Tip:

Important storytelling techniques include the use of voice (words and sound effects), facial expression and bodily gesture, mime, pace, repetition, rhythm, elaboration, exaggeration and – most of all – engagement with the audience.

videos of storytelling and encourage the children to identify techniques they could use in their own stories.

Rather than learning stories by rote pupils should identify key images and important moments, and retell the story in their own words. *Still images* can be used to mark out those key moments, as can drawing storyboards and story maps or (for younger children) sorting pictures into the right order. It is well worth playing some games to develop oral skills and get the creative juices flowing. These can help to develop vocabulary, story-making and storytelling techniques.

Getting Started

Begin with some word association games like *Word Tennis* (see below) and *One word at a time* stories. Move on to the students making up their own stories as a class or in groups. Pie Corbett (2009, p.61) suggests that children make up whacky excuses for being late and they can have great fun with this: ask small groups to concoct various preposterous excuses to explain why they were late that day and to make sure that each group knows all the reasons. Then ask the group to convincingly explain the story to yourself and the rest of the class. Ask questions to draw out the details and before you know it they will be making up and telling an exciting and original adventure story. Group storytelling works particularly well with mixed-ability pupils.

 Tip:

Word Tennis

In this word-association game, pupils have to keep thinking up words in a chosen category and 'bat' them to each other. Whoever repeats a word or can't think of one is out, and somebody else takes his or her place. You can demonstrate with two students and then play it in pairs or teams of four or five students. Each team should form a line facing another team. The two students at the head of each line play each other until one of them can't think of a word – or repeats an earlier word. That person goes to the back of the line and the next student takes their place.

Categories can include colours, fruit, sea creatures, flavours of ice cream, fairy tale characters, sports, capital cities, adverbs, adjectives and so on. Change the categories as often as you need to maintain interest. Students will soon come up with their own interesting suggestions for new categories.

Storytelling for very young children

The Helicopter Technique, invented by Vivian Gussin Paley (1990), is a powerful method of involving children in telling and acting out their own stories. Children as young as two and upward are asked to tell a story to an adult, who writes it down for them. When the whole class have told their stories, the children act out each story with the child who wrote the story taking one of the lead roles. This strategy has been developed in the UK by *MakeBelieve Arts* who provide training, books and videos (see *Further Resources*).

Examples

The following storytelling ideas can be worked on in groups as well as individually as pupils gain more confidence.

Geography

★ Tell stories about survival in a harsh environment such as a mountain, desert or icescape.

★ An animal in a threatened habitat tells its story.

History

★ Each pupil brings in a man-made object relating to family history – recent or distant. They tell the story of the artefact, make *still images* or a *mime* showing the object in use and research it for the class museum.

★ Describe an important event from the point of view of a bystander.

Literacy, Speaking and Listening

★ With younger children, practice retelling stories with them. Story maps and story sacks can help with this.

★ As they develop confidence, encourage pupils to tell the story in groups and pairs – making the storytelling more exciting each time.

★ Children can retell a well-known story in their own style, changing the ending or adding a modern twist. Inspirational written examples include: *The Three Little Wolves and the Big Bad Pig* (Trivizas 2003) and *The Paper Bag Princess* (Munsch 1980).

★ When children are familiar with a story, play *rumours* to help them pass on snippets of the story as they walk round the room.

★ Retell the same story from the point of view of different characters.

★ Pupils can recount stories about funny things that have happened to them or other people they know.

★ Children collect and record stories from friends and extended family members.

★ Small groups of children will enjoy practicing stories to tell or perform to other classes.

★ Use *narration* alongside *improvisation* to present a story dramatically.

★ Tell a story of the time you played a trick on somebody – or when you were tricked.

★ Describe what really happened in an amusing family photo.

★ Get inspiration for a story by throwing dice with *Rory's Story Cubes*[3].

Science

★ A week (or year) in the life of a growing plant.

★ The life cycle of a butterfly or a frog.

★ The effect of gravity and heat on a snowflake.

★ A story to illustrate that every action has an equal and opposite reaction or to compare the speed of light with the speed of sound.

See also: *Bags and Boxes, Flashbacks, Guided Tour, Living Newspaper, Narration, One Word at a Time, Open and Close, Soundscapes, Visualisation.*

---

[3] www.storycubes.com

Narration (by the teacher)

R 1 2 | Whole Class | 5 minutes +

Storytelling used by the teacher to shape the drama.

Why use it?

The teacher may use narration to develop a whole class drama through the familiar technique of storytelling; setting the scene, speeding up or slowing down events, introducing new information, summarising what has happened and encouraging reflection. The children may simply listen, act out the story as it is told or incorporate the information into their own drama work. Narration can set the stage for *teacher in role* or lead the students into occupational *mime, improvisation* or other drama activity.

How do you do it?

Any time you want to inject atmosphere or move the action forward, narration is a valuable tool. You can tell a story off the top of your head or read aloud a piece of literature, an historical account or other descriptive text. Evocative and active language should be used so that students are encouraged to think about each of their senses and become more immersed in the drama.

In this section we focus on using narration while the students are active during the drama. For an explanation of how to use narration to initially set the scene see *Visualisation.* Both approaches can be used together.

Examples

Setting the scene

★   In the Workhouse: *You are lying in bed; it's cold and you can hear other children coughing in the darkness. Slowly you pull back the blanket, get out of bed and put on a rough cotton smock. Imagine how the wooden floor feels under your bare feet…*

★ 'The Nightingale' by Hans Christian Anderson: *With your eyes closed, visualise the Emperor's garden and palace. Try to see, hear and smell the flowers with silver bells in your mind. What else can you see in the garden? Now open your eyes and you can see the royal garden around you. Get into a space on your own and imagine that you are in one of your favourite parts of the garden. You are one of the royal gardeners and have some jobs to do in that spot. Begin to mime the activities you are involved in...*

Moving the drama on

★ *Then suddenly the whole crowd fell silent. The King stood up on the balcony and began to speak: "My dear citizens…"* (Leading into **teacher in role**.)

Summarising what has happened

★ *James unpacked his suitcase and carefully placed his clothes in the drawer. He lay down on the bed and thought about what had happened during the last few days from the time he was evacuated from Manchester to his arrival in the village of Sudbury….*

Encouraging reflection

★ *As you pull on the heavy oars the ship rocks from side to side. You hear the groans of other soldiers as they row. You wonder to yourself what Troy is like and what will happen when you get there. Where will you set up camp? How long will you fight for? Will you be able to rescue Helen? Turn to your partner and discuss what is going through your mind.*

See also: *Guided Tour, Mime, One Word at a Time, Storytelling, Visualisation, Whoosh!*

Narration (by the students) 12

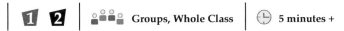 1 2 | Groups, Whole Class | 5 minutes +

Storytelling used by the students to structure their performance.

Why use it?

Students can use narration to introduce a performance, link scenes together, give information or comment on the action and the characters.

How do you do it?

Narration may be used in many ways as part of a performance. The narrator can be separate from the performers – or characters in a scene may narrate by speaking directly to the audience. Usually the characters behave as though they can't see the narrator or hear what is being said, although you can have fun breaking these rules.

Examples

★ The narrator introduces and links scenes.

★ Two narrators take it in turns to tell the story from contrasting viewpoints.

★ Characters begin by telling a story and then move into performance once they have set the scene.

★ All the actors narrate the story between them, perhaps using *one word at a time* or choral speaking.

★ The narrator makes up or tells a story while the other students improvise what is being described. The narrator can leave space for the characters to speak to each other or the action can be silent.

See also: *Guided Tour, One Word at a Time, Storytelling, Visualisation.*

Visualisation

  Whole Class | 10 minutes +

> Students close their eyes to visualise images, stories and places while listening to narration, storytelling, poetry or music.

Why use it?

Visualisation harnesses the imagination to enable children to travel to different places in their mind's eye. It can be used to provide focus at the beginning of a drama session or to deepen involvement during a lesson. It helps to create atmosphere prior to telling a story or setting up an *improvisation*.

How do you do it?

Visualisation can be carried out while children listen to *narration*, *storytelling*, poetry or music. The children sit or lie down on the floor and may close their eyes. The teacher uses sensory language to describe a place, environment or atmosphere so that pupils can imagine what they see, touch, hear, smell and taste. You may choose to play music or sound effects whilst narrating.

As a development you can get feedback during the visualisation by using *thought tracking* - tap children on the shoulder and ask them to describe what they are imagining so that their ideas become part of the experience. Afterwards you can ask for pupils' responses such as colours, images or stories that came to mind. This often leads to a rich variety of responses. The depth of mental imagery evoked through visualisation can also create invaluable opportunities for a variety of writing tasks and visual art activities.

Examples

Geography

★ Narrate a journey on a magic carpet that flies the children to another country. It can take them to different regions so that they imagine mountains, rivers, seas, vegetation and so on. The carpet can fly them high above the land or down to the ground to provide different perspectives. Sound effects and music will enhance the experience. Make sure you bring them home afterwards!

★ Record sound effects from places you travel to and see if the children can identify where they are – or use a pre-recorded soundtrack.

★ Groups of children rehearse *soundscapes* to represent particular places for the rest of the class to listen to as an aid to visualisation.

History

★ Read War poetry aloud and lead onto sculpting group *tableaux*.

★ The Anglo-Saxons: *Imagine a country covered in thick forests of oak trees where you may find deer, wolves, foxes and badgers. Narrow roads run through the forests connecting village to village. A horse and cart rattles along one of these roads, finally drawing into the centre of a village. All around are small wooden huts thatched with straw, with wisps of smoke rising from each one. Sounds can be heard of adults cooking and chopping wood and children feeding the pigs, sheep and cattle. From one of the huts comes the sound of a hammer hitting molten iron on an anvil...*

Literacy

★ Before telling a story from another country, play some indigenous music and ask students what images, colours and stories came to mind.

★ Try listening to extracts of descriptive or narrative poetry and prose with your eyes shut, for example *The Highwayman* by Alfred Noyes, *The Listeners* by Walter De La Mare, *The Lady of Shalott* by Tennyson, *Blackberry-Picking* by Seamus Heaney, *Wind* and animal poems by Ted Hughes, *The Tyre* by Simon Armitage or passages from Shakespeare and Dickens.

★ Encourage children to write abstract word collages in free verse. Use these as a stimulus for other children to listen to. Their abstract nature will be open to wider interpretation.

See also: *Guided Tour, Narration, Soundscapes, Storytelling.*

Guided Tour 14

1 **2** | Groups, Whole Class | 10 minutes +

An orally described journey by the teacher or children – or a sensory tour where one student leads a blindfolded partner while describing the imaginary surroundings.

Why use it?

Through the use of language and imagination the classroom, drama space or school field can become another environment anywhere in the world at any point in time. The activity encourages speaking and listening skills and helps to develop descriptive and instructional language, sensory awareness, listening, cooperation and storytelling skills.

"And just to your left is a tarantula…"

How do you do it?

The teacher – or groups of children – discuss and prepare an imaginary guided tour of a particular place or event. While the journey is being described the rest of the class close their eyes and listen. Pupils can read written ideas from their books but should ultimately be encouraged to develop their storytelling skills by improvising the description.

An active version of the strategy involves working in pairs or threes. One person is blindfolded (or has their eyes closed) while the other partner(s) describes the imaginary scene and carefully leads the student around the space. Model the activity with one pair or group of three first so that students can be reminded about safety issues. The leaders may guide using touch or just by using words. It can be helpful to play some simple trust games beforehand such as *Blind Walk* (Farmer 2007) or the *Mirror Exercise (p.80)*. If it is a large class then just have a few pairs or groups at a time – the rest of the class will enjoy watching and listening.

As well as using sensory language, the leader can describe imaginary (or real) obstacles that their partner has to step over, through, around or under. Experiment with asking the blindfolded partner to feel textures or objects to heighten the experience. These could be objects which are already part of the space or which have been carefully selected according to the theme. Because you are relying on children's imaginations you can be quite creative – part of a climbing frame could be a prison bar or the leaf of a potted plant could be a rainforest plant (actually it probably is).

You may like to play appropriate background sound effects and can begin with some atmospheric "magical" music to transport the children to the new time or place. *Soundscape* and *visualisation* can easily be combined with this technique. Afterwards students can discuss what they encountered on their journey.

Further development: Write stories, draw pictures and maps of the imagined journey. Engage a child as a sound engineer to record the account of the guided tour as it is being told. This can be played back later and used as a stimulus for other activity.

Examples

Geography

★ An Amazonian rainforest.

★ A busy city in India.

★ A visit to another planet.

★ The Great Barrier Reef from the point of view of an octopus.

★ A summer meadow from the view of a field mouse or fox.

History

★ A tour around a pyramid-building site in Ancient Egypt.

★ A visit to a Norman castle.

★ An ant crawling around the table at a Tudor banquet.

★ An inspection of a hospital in the Crimean war.

Literacy

★ A guided tour around any story location is a novel way to help children remember the details – or to add their own. Children could describe a journey through *Willy Wonka's* chocolate factory or *Hogwart's School of Witchcraft and Wizardry*.

Science

★ A visit to a rabbit warren.

★ A tour through an anthill.

★ A blood cell travelling through the human circulatory system.

See also: *Narration, Soundscape, Storytelling, Visualisation.*

One Word at a Time $\boxed{15}$

1 **2** | Pairs, Groups, Whole Class | 🕐 10 minutes +

Students tell a story by taking it in turns to speak one word at a time.

Why use it?

Speaking one word at a time enables children to quickly improvise a collective story, develop their storytelling and listening skills and learn to value one another's ideas. It can also be used as a novel way of narrating alongside a performance.

How do you do it?

The rule is simple – students add just one word to the story when it is their turn. This works best if children are sitting in a circle but can also be done at desks in the classroom. An easy way to begin is with the first four people saying: "Once – Upon – A – Time". The story can continue organically after this: "There – Was…" and so on.

To begin with children will need more support to keep the story flowing and you will occasionally have to remind them of what has been said previously. Sometimes it will be obvious when a sentence should end while at other times it may help for the teacher to say "full stop". Eventually children may start saying this for themselves but eventually the story should flow without the need to mention punctuation.

Don't be too ambitious to begin with – just a few sentences are quite an achievement. Encourage students to keep their thoughts free flowing so that they don't pre-empt what is coming or force the story in a particular direction. As children become more used to the technique you can set a theme, such as a ghost story or place the story in a particular environment, such as on a mountain-side.

Making up a story with a contribution from everybody in the class can be a good way to begin. Working in pairs has the advantage that children don't have to wait long to have their go but it does require them to be able to come up with words more spontaneously. For this reason working in small groups is probably the best method for most children.

If you have the space an enjoyable variation is to throw a ball around the circle in any order. Each person adds a word before throwing the ball to the next person. This is a good way of maintaining alertness, although you should make sure everyone is included. One word at a time can also be used to improvise a narrative alongside action – see *Narration (by the students)*.

See also: *Improvisation, Narration, Storytelling.*

Bags and Boxes 16

| R 1 2 | Groups, Whole Class | 15 minutes + |

Objects in a bag or box are used to support storytelling and to stimulate creative and narrative skills.

Why use it?

Story sacks, character bags and story boxes offer exciting ways to stimulate imaginative thought and action as well as speaking, listening and observational skills. *Story bags* can support the telling of a story or spark off a new one. They can even be empty, waiting for the children's imagination to fill them. A *character bag* contains objects that give clues about the owner – perhaps a character from an existing story, from history or a newly invented personality.

How do you do it?

You can use any container, but a sack or bag ensures there is a surprise element, as students can't see the objects before they are removed. On the other hand a box is useful if you wish the pupils to see all the objects more easily.

 Tip:

Choosing Objects

Multisensory: textures, colours, smells, tastes and sounds
Objects that make sounds related to the story
Unusual or ambiguous objects that can be used in many ways

Story Bags and Boxes

There are many ways you can use a story sack and here are just a few to get you going.

(i) **Story Sacks:** The bag contains significant objects related to a story such as puppets, costumes and props. These are revealed as the story is told and can be passed around. Students can participate by playing with puppets or taking on different roles. You can buy ready-made kits for well-known stories or simply make your own. Groups of children can retell stories using story sacks or collect appropriate objects for tales of their own.

(ii) **Fill the Bag:** The bag is empty but is passed around the circle as each child names and mimes the item they are putting into it. For example, students imagine what they might need to take on a journey as an archaeologist, explorer or character from a story. This can lead on to creative writing and *improvisation*.

(iii) **Magic Box:** You can carry out this activity without any props at all. An invisible "magic" box is passed around the circle and each student takes it in turn to open the box and remove an imaginary item. They show what it is by miming its use while everybody else tries to guess it. They replace the mimed object, close the box and pass it on to the next person. The objects can be realistic, like a cat or a book; or magical, like a cloak of invisibility or a magic carpet. They could be related to a story that is being told.

(iv)   ***Story Box:*** A box is used to keep a number of objects related to a story or theme over a period of time. As the class learns more about the story / theme they can choose symbolic items to add to the collection – or remove items if they don't think they are relevant. During the project they can handle the objects and use them to tell part or all of the story to each other.

Character Bag

Select a number of items relating to a character and place them in a bag – one that the character would have been likely to own. This can be introduced in the context of the children acting as detectives – ask them to help you find out who the bag belonged to. Show them each object one by one or pass them round for examination. Invite suggestions about the character and notice how these develop as each object is revealed. The character and story can be developed using drama strategies such as ***role on the wall***, ***still images*** or ***improvisation*** as well as ***storytelling***, creative writing and artwork.

★   Useful containers include: beach bag, briefcase, duffel bag, handbag, hessian sack, rucksack, satchel, shoe-box, shopping bag, suitcase

★   Objects can include: personal possessions, photos, diary, letters, tickets, toys, tools, keys

Examples

History

★   Use objects in a bag to launch a topic – for example a suitcase containing children's clothes and toys could launch a project on refugees.

★   Students place an imaginary object into a time capsule to let people of the future know what is important to them. They can also do this in role as people from any era – what would Romans, Victorians, ancient Mayans or Sumerians choose to be remembered by?

Literacy

★   To kick off a detective story go into role as a police officer and introduce objects in plastic bags "found at the scene of the crime" or a bag belonging to one of the suspects containing some tantalising artefacts.

See also: ***Object Theatre, Role on the Wall, Ritual, Role Play, Speaking Objects, Storytelling.***

Physical Strategies

Physical drama strategies enable students to explore themes and create meaning by intuitively 'thinking with their bodies'. This non-verbal approach appeals to a wide range of pupils and can easily lead onto speaking and listening activities.

In this section:

- Still Images and Freeze-Frames

- Tableaux

- Sculpting

- Ten Second Objects

- Speaking Objects

- Mime

- Essence Machines

Still Images & Freeze-Frames 17

   Pairs, Groups, Whole Class | 5 minutes +

> Still images or freeze-frames are physical shapes created by individuals or groups using their bodies.

Why use it?

Still images and *freeze-frames* provide an immediate way of creating drama and are easily accessible to all age groups. No one has lines to learn or has to 'act' in front of others. As no speaking is involved in presenting the images the approach appeals to pupils who are less verbally confident, preparing the ground for moving on to the improvised word. Using the body to make shapes encourages awareness of physical communication and body language. Still images can be used to represent people or objects as well as abstract concepts like emotions and atmospheres.

Even though the technique can be learnt and implemented very quickly, it is remarkably versatile and can be used to explore issues, attitudes and emotions, to invent a new story or illustrate an existing one and to demonstrate learning of a concept. This active and visually based approach can be particularly helpful for pupils who are usually reluctant to write. Still images enable students to explore their own feelings and experiences in a less forbidding way than that offered by improvisational techniques.

 Tip:

Questions to ask characters in a still image

What are you thinking?
What do you wish for?
How do you feel about other people around you?
What do you want to tell other people in the tableau?

Questions to ask students about a still image

What do we know from looking at the image?
What do we think might be true?
What would we like to know more about?

Prompts for commenting on still images

I can see ...
I wonder ...
I imagine ...

How do you do it?

Still images require individuals or groups to devise shapes through activity and discussion. *Freeze-frames* are made by stopping the action in an improvised or rehearsed scene to clarify, reflect, explore issues and slow things down. This can be done by simply calling "Freeze!" while students are running through a scene. It can be explained to children that it is like pressing the pause button on a remote control. In fact you can use an imaginary or real remote control for a bit of fun – which can develop into *flash forwards* and *flashback*. Students may invent spoken or written captions for their images. Alternatively members of the audience can suggest a caption for a group image.

You can review learning in any subject area by dividing the students into groups and asking them to discuss and create still images to summarise concepts they have been learning about. This works particularly well with *sculpting*. With older students *image theatre* can be used to create physical images in response to a given theme such as bullying. Students stand in a circle and each makes an image quickly without too much pre-thought. They are then invited to step into the centre of the circle and remake their image. Other students add in their own still images. This can lead to an abstract group image or **tableau** that is brought alive through **thought tracking** or by adding sound or movement.[4]

 Tip:

> *When developing and showing work, encourage pupils to look at how they can use facial expression and body postures to communicate their ideas as well as exploring physical levels (low, medium and high) and proximity (distance from one another).*

Examples

History

★ Groups create statues to commemorate an important historical event – representing objects as well as people.

Literacy

★ Groups can tell a story by using three images to create a beginning, middle and end.

★ Improve vocabulary skills by asking students to illustrate a word or phrase in a story using a still image.

★ *Collective storyboarding*: A small group makes an image on a theme. Ask the class what could happen next and to help the group create the next image. Lead on to groups making their own physical storyboards.

★ One child thinks of a character from a story and makes a still image which the others try to guess. Whoever guesses correctly enters the space and adds an image – another character or an object. When enough images have been added the scene can be brought to life.

★ Groups prepare and share a still image of a favourite moment in a story. Next they rehearse and show a short scene – beginning with the still image and ending with a freeze-frame.

---

[4] Further image theatre approaches can be found in *The Rainbow of Desire* (Boal 1995).

★ Children can photograph or video each group's sequence of images to provide a ready-made storyboard. This can be developed into creative writing or cartoons with speech-bubbles. These can be enhanced using comic creation software such as *Comic Life*[5].

★ Letters of the alphabet – give a small group of children a camera and ask them to take photos of each other making the shapes of different letters. The photos can later be used to spell words or to make an alphabet to display on the wall.

★ Fun can be had making group objects that turn from one thing into something else – for example Cinderella's pumpkin turns into a coach, mice into horses, a rat into a coachman, and lizards into footmen.

Poetry

★ Divide the class into pairs and give each a line or two from a poem. Ask them to devise still images to represent any significant words and phrases. If they create more than one image for their lines they can find a way of moving between them to create a piece of movement or dance. The same approach can be used for exploring a speech from Shakespeare.

Science

★ In pairs make a still image of an animal and a food the animal likes to eat.

★ In groups develop a series of images showing the process of metamorphosis (e.g. caterpillar to butterfly or frogspawn to frog).

★ Make a sequence of images showing three healthy actions (for example cleaning teeth or going for a jog) then three unhealthy actions (such as eating ice-cream or driving a car instead of walking).

See also: *Flashbacks and Flash Forwards, Marking the Moment, Open and Close, Sculpting, Speaking Objects, Tableaux, Ten Second Objects, Thought Tracking.*

---

[5] Available from www.plasq.com

Tableaux 18

  |  Groups, Whole Class | 🕐 10 minutes +

> Students make still images with their bodies to represent a scene.

Why use it?

A tableau can be used to quickly establish a scene that involves several characters. Because there is no movement, a tableau is easier to manage than a whole-group improvisation, yet can easily lead into extended drama activities. Tableaux can be brought to life with a simple click of the fingers. They can be used to explore a particular moment in a story or drama, or to replicate images from a picture for deeper analysis.

How do you do it?

Students stand in a circle and a theme is given. One by one they step into the space and establish *still images* in relation to one another until the tableau is complete. As a development *thought tracking* can be used to find out more about each of the characters. The scene can be brought to life through *improvisation* with the teacher clapping her hands to signal the beginning and end of the action. Alternatively the teacher can step into the scene in role – at which point the characters come to life.

Once students are familiar with creating tableaux they can work in small groups on different aspects of a theme. The class can discuss each group's tableau in turn mentioning what they can see happening, what they would like to know more about and what they think could happen next. Afterwards each group can comment on how these viewpoints compared with their initial intentions.

A series of tableaux can be created as a useful way to develop visually interesting performances with the optional addition of a narrator, who can be telling a story or making a commentary. If groups are creating a series of tableaux you can ask them to find a way of making transitions from one tableau to the next (see *Dance and Movement* below). Tableaux can also be sculpted by students *(p.71)*.

Examples

Art/History

★   Pupils look carefully at a painting or illustration of a historical scene depicting a range of characters. This can be projected onto the wall to make it life-size. One by one students step forward to make still images representing people in the painting, as accurately as possible. The tableau can be brought to life through mime or improvisation. Suitable artists include Pieter Brueghel, William Hogarth, Ford Madox Brown and L.S. Lowry.

Dance and Movement

★   Movement skills can be developed once groups have created a series of tableaux. Ask them to find a fluid way of moving from one picture to the next to create a movement sequence. Adding music can help to encourage expressive movement and create atmosphere. It is worth experimenting with the effect of playing different types of music for the same sequence ranging from upbeat instrumental music to a theme from a horror or suspense movie.

Environmental Studies

★ Groups make a tableau showing a problem in the world today and share it with the class. Next they devise a tableau depicting the ideal solution. They can make this into a story that they tell, act out or write. Alternatively they can design a poster based on the tableau.

Geography

★ Create a postcard image of another country. This could include famous buildings (like the pyramids or the Great Wall of China, a landscape (like the desert or mountains) or everyday cultural activities. Groups can make up a message that would be written on the postcard and speak it between them *one word at a time*. Working in pairs or groups, students can design and make actual postcards afterwards and pin them to a world map.

★ Make a tableau for a postcard sent by an animal that has gone on holiday to a place with the "wrong" environment such as a giraffe visiting the North Pole or a penguin in Jamaica. Add a narrated message from the animal.

★ Make a travellers' guide to your hometown featuring tableaux of important places and landmarks along with a spoken commentary.

History

★ Children look at a painting of Florence Nightingale at Scutari hospital. Small groups make tableaux of areas of the painting then work on revised versions of the images, highlighting improvements that could be made.

★ Text extracts describing episodes of a historical event are given out. Groups prepare tableaux of these and they are presented in sequence. Can the students work out the whole story?

★ Small groups are given alternative newspaper reports of the same incident (or differing accounts of an historical event) and asked to produce as accurate a tableau as possible. This can be used to examine how events may be communicated differently according to the observer's point of view. Newspaper headlines can be spoken or written for the individual images.

★ The Bayeux Tapestry or ancient Greek friezes and vase paintings can be used for inspiration.

★ Groups create a tableau based around a famous historical character which other students have to guess.

Literacy

★ Invite children to invent pictures for a story as you read it to them, stopping at key points to do so. Alternatively, they can listen to a story all the way through and then small groups can create images for a series of key moments. Each group can show their image in turn as you re-tell the story to the whole class.

★ Groups can be assigned an epic poem or story such as *Beowulf*, *Jabberwocky*, the *Odyssey* or the *Ramayana*. They select key points and create a sequence of tableaux to illustrate these. When they share the results, compare which key points each group has selected and why. The session can be followed up with an art activity where pupils illustrate the tableaux using a variety of materials and techniques.

★ Create alternative illustrations for a storybook or textbook using photographs of tableaux made by students.

★ Create a dream sequence for a character from a story. Add evocative repeated words and sounds. Move slowly from one tableau to the next with atmospheric music playing in the background.

Personal and Social Education

★ Be abstract – use tableaux to explore emotions such as anger, embarrassment, suspicion or surprise; or concepts such as friendship, fear, creativity or ignorance.

Science

★ In groups, one student plays the part of a scientist presenting a slide show about a particular topic, such as the extinction of the dinosaurs. The other group members have to jump into position to make a *tableau* for each slide when the scientist presses an imaginary remote-control[6].

Just for Fun

★ For a more light-hearted activity, groups secretly devise a tableau (in a different room) on a specific theme such as favourite books and movies, famous locations and well-known historical events. The other students then try and guess what the tableau represents (using *thought-tracking* if they get stuck).

---

[6] Adapted from 'Slide Show' in *Unscripted Learning* (Lobman and Lundquist 2007)

Sculpting

1 **2** | Groups, Whole Class | 10 minutes +

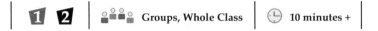

Students model each other into shapes to represent characters or objects.

Why use it?

Sculpting enables children to cooperate in producing *still images* and *tableaux*. One advantage is that it can be easier to help someone else make a shape than to produce it with your own body. Additionally your partner is likely to mould you into positions that you wouldn't have thought of yourself. Sculpting is enjoyably unpredictable for the person being shaped.

How do you do it?

Sculpting can be done in pairs or in groups where one person moulds the others or the whole group moulds one person. Begin in twos: one person is the sculptor who has to mould their partner (the block of clay) into a statue linked to a chosen theme. The person being sculpted stands in a neutral position and the sculptor moves them carefully into a new shape. This is normally done without talking. Students may not wish to have their faces moulded so the sculptor can show the required facial expression by demonstrating it using their own face.

When they are finished the sculptors can walk around the "exhibition" and try to guess what the statues represent. It can be fun for the sculptors to make up captions or titles for the sculpture – these can be written or spoken. The sculpture exhibition can be themed to suit a topic – such as "Gods and Goddesses of Ancient Greece" or "Victorian Inventions".

It is not easy to stand still for a long period so when it is time to share work, children can sit down and watch while each pair or group takes it in turns to show how they made their finished image including the moulding process (this shouldn't take as long as it did the first time around).

Examples

★ Themes can range from hobbies and occupations to animals, emotions, famous people, characters from a story and of course objects.

★ Sculpting a child into the pose of a character can help when rehearsing a play.

★ All of the ideas from the sections on *Still Images* and *Tableaux* can be used for sculpting.

Ten Second Objects 20

| **1** **2** | Groups, Whole Class | 5 minutes + |

Groups of students use their bodies to quickly make an overall physical shape.

Why use it?

Ten second objects help children to work instinctively, cooperatively and creatively while developing physical awareness. This versatile cross-curricular technique can be used for generating ideas, reviewing learning or as an introduction to a theme. Perhaps the best thing about the strategy is that children have little time to talk – or argue – and as a result the ideas are produced quickly and creatively.

How do you do it?

Divide the class into small groups of around 4 - 6 students. When you call out the name of an object all the groups have to make its shape out of their own bodies, joining together in different ways while you count down slowly from ten to zero. Usually every group will find a different way of forming the object.

Encourage groups to observe how they can use different levels with their body shapes, i.e. high, medium and low. Once students get the hang of this activity they can be given a couple of minutes to devise an object of their own that the rest of the class try to guess. They can add movement and sounds if appropriate (younger children will tend to do this anyway).

Just about any object can be made in this way, including objects from a theme you are exploring, a play you are rehearsing, a story you have told or are about to tell. Objects can be any shape or size and can include locations, environments, letters of the alphabet, words, numbers and so on. You may want to have a camera handy as many of the shapes will look quite ingenious and will serve as a reminder of the learning experience if displayed on the wall.

Here are some popular ideas to get you started: a car, a steam locomotive, a cuckoo clock, a fried breakfast, a washing machine, a volcano.

Examples

Geography

★ A tornado. A volcano. A rainforest. A mountain rescue scene. A road sign. The Taj Mahal, the Eiffel Tower, the Great Pyramid or any famous landmark. The London or New York skyline.

History

★ A dinosaur. An ammonite. Stonehenge. The Coliseum. A Viking longship. A medieval castle. Victorian inventions and toys. A World War II gas mask. A Doodlebug. An item seen during a recent trip to a museum.

Literacy and language learning

★ Spell words with everybody making the shape of a different letter.

★ Consolidate new vocabulary by making shapes of the objects concerned.

Maths

★ Two and three-dimensional shapes.

★ Number shapes.

★ Clocks and times.

★ Operators such as minus, plus, multiply, percentage, equals.

★ Call out a sum and see if children can make the answer by making shapes of numbers.

Music

★ A rock group. A treble clef. Individual musical instruments such as a piano, guitar, flute, drum set – or a French horn if you are feeling particularly ambitious.

Performance

★ You can use the shapes created as a quick way into creating ideas for physical theatre.

Science

★ Snowflakes and crystal patterns.

★ An octopus. A scorpion. A bird's nest.

★ Bridge structures. Levers and pulleys.

★ Food types – ask each group to make a food of a different type, e.g. protein, carbohydrate, fat (these could be on cards).

★ Parts of the body.

★ A light bulb.

★ An object related to air resistance such as a feather or parachute.

★ Something made of ice (then ask them to melt).

Speaking Objects 21

     Pairs, Groups, Whole Class   10 minutes +

> Students make the shapes of objects and speak aloud what they might be observing and feeling.

Why use it?

Speaking as an object enables students to gain a deeper understanding of a situation, character or object by seeing it from an unusual viewpoint. It encourages pupils to understand and respect the nature of physical objects. The approach combines still images and thought tracking. (*Speaking Object* can also be used to describe a symbolic or sacred object passed around a group enabling one person at a time to speak - like a Native American talking stick.)

How do you do it?

If working in pairs and small groups, students can be related objects –
such as a pair of shoes or a box of toys. When working as a whole class,
pupils can become speaking objects in a particular place such as furniture
in a living room or items in a shop window. Once the theme has been set
students are invited to step into a circle and make a shape one at a time,
stating the object they represent. Some students can remain outside the
space in order to ask questions of the objects.

Examples

The following activities can be done in pairs, small groups or as a whole
class activity.

History

★ In *Away From Home (p.141)*, an evacuee is deciding what to pack in a
suitcase while the objects explain why she needs them with her.

★ Pupils pretend to be Anglo-Saxon artefacts found in a burial mound
and describe what they might have been used for.

★ Pupils create artefacts that were part of the Great Exhibition of 1851
and the teacher takes the role of a visitor interacting with each exhibit.

Geography/Maths

★ Groups make market stalls representing different countries and
cultures. Each group decides on the produce and cultural artefacts to
have on their stall and how much they will cost. (This can involve some
internet/library research if required.) The teacher visits each stall and
the children as objects try to sell themselves to her. She should "buy"
the most persuasive objects from each stall. At the end the class can
work out how much she spent in total. Older students can calculate
how many air miles the objects may have travelled.

★ The *teacher in role* explains that she is going on a journey to a particular
environment, such as snowy mountains. Each group decides on
essential items to take on the trip and makes shapes of the objects they
have chosen. The teacher visits each group in turn explaining that she
can only take one item from each group. Each speaking object tries to
persuade the teacher how important they are and why she should take
them with her without saying the name of the object. For example, a
torch might say, "You will need me if you are sleeping in a cave and
you want to check if there are wild animals in there." The rest of the

class try to guess the object and the teacher decides which object from each group she is persuaded to take with her.

Literacy

★ Students can become speaking objects to show their understanding of a story, to comment on events and characters or to take the drama forward. For example, they can be household objects discussing what they think of *Cinderella* and her sisters *(p.135)*, forest plants and animals in *The Gruffalo (p.130)* or the bridge in the *Three Billy Goats Gruff*.

Personal and Social Education

★ A pencil or book explains what it feels like to be dropped on the floor and forgotten.

Science

★ Pupils play different types of food in a supermarket with each one trying to persuade the teacher that they are either the tastiest or the healthiest – or both!

★ One child in a group is a scientist and the others together make an object that changes its physical nature. The scientist comments on the object while it changes – for example a piece of bread in a toaster, an egg that is broken and fried, a seed growing into a plant, a fizzy drink can that is opened or a melting ice-lolly. As well as moving to show the changes the object can comment on what is taking place and how it feels. Students can turn these into amusing lecture/demonstrations.

Speaking and Listening

★ In small groups students select a particular room in a building and which objects they will represent, for example instruments in a doctor's surgery. The teacher or a student in role enters the room and asks each object questions to find out what and where they are. This can also be used for historical buildings and places.

★ Pupils make the shapes of works of art in a gallery and explain to visitors why they think they are the most creative or original.

★ Objects in a second-hand shop talk about where they used to live and who used to own them.

Mime  22

| R 1 2 | 👥 Pairs, Groups, Whole Class | 🕐 10 minutes + |

> The use of physical movement to imaginatively explore activities in role or to communicate stories and characters.

Why use it?

Mime is a natural part of children's play and an integral part of dramatic activity. It deepens pupils' engagement in the make-believe, particularly appealing to kinaesthetic learners. Mime enables students to develop precision and clarity in their movement which in turn helps their communication and performance skills.

How do you do it?

Symbolic movement occurs naturally within dramatic activity, whether a child is fighting a monster, climbing a mountain or mixing ingredients for a cake. *Occupational mime* helps children deepen their identification with the imagined physical world. You can initiate this by using **narration** to help pupils picture a scene in their minds *(p.49)*. Occupational activities might include archaeologists unearthing a find, farmworkers harvesting crops or Victorian children working in a coal mine. It is important that mime is used to enable students to develop their ideas rather than just reproduce narrated action.

Mimed action naturally occurs when children play and is a natural part of *improvisation* and *storytelling*. When a group of children tell a story some will instinctively "act it out" while the others narrate. Using mimed gestures while storytelling helps the audience visualise what is happening. The *mirror exercise* (see next page) is excellent practice for encouraging children to watch and copy each other's movements.

There are no hard and fast rules about mime. In performance it is traditionally considered to be silent but mime can feature sound effects,

◉ Tip:

Mirror Exercise

Two partners face each other. One of them begins by making a slow and smooth movement that the other should try to copy simultaneously. Begin with hand and arm movements. When you feel more confident start to move other parts of your body and to explore different levels by sitting down and standing up for example. After a short time the teacher can give a signal so that the leading swaps over. Encourage students to be accurate and to keep the flow of movement each time there is a changeover. Try giving a theme such as toys, animals or getting ready for school.

narration, music and (sometimes) even speech. Slow-motion mime is valuable for highlighting crucial moments of the drama or for showing an act of aggression in a stylised form.

Examples

History

★ Look carefully at a photo or painting from history then make a *tableau* and bring it alive through mimed movement.

★ Each group is given a card with an illustration and/or description of a Victorian invention. They devise a mimed representation of it for the other groups to guess. As an extension they could also devise a fictional invention and the others have to guess which invention actually existed.

Literacy

★ Read part of a story then ask the students to mime what they think happens next.

★ Read a story that the children enact simultaneously. Following this they can devise scenes to show what they think happens next.

Science

★ Use mime to explore physical forces such as gravity, friction or magnetism, or to represent the action of molecules, planets, volcanoes and electrical circuits.

★ Develop group mimes showing typical behaviour of an animal species and add a television-style commentary.

★ Represent an animated 3D model of food passing through the digestive system using the whole class.

★ Younger children can choose animals to mime that the others have to guess.

See also: *Improvisation, Essence Machines, Marking the Moment, Ten Second Objects.*

Essence Machines $\boxed{23}$

1 **2** | 👥 **Groups, Whole Class** | 🕐 **10 minutes +**

Students work together to make repeating sounds and movements based on a theme – producing a machine-like effect.

Why use it?

The activity enables the group to quickly create a lively dramatic performance including as many students as wish to take part. Essence machines can be a good starting point for generating ideas and creativity, or a snapshot of where the group is at in their learning.

How do you do it?

Students are asked to invent a short repeating action with words or sounds, linked to a selected theme. The first person starts off in the centre of a circle and repeats their sound (or phrase) and action over and over. One by one others step in, finding a suitable way to link their movement and sounds. Each student should interact with at least one other person in the group to give the overall effect of a human machine. This should involve interconnecting movements and sounds.

With a larger group there will come a point when you have enough participants – and many students will enjoy just watching the machine. Those who didn't have a turn can go first next time. Partly as a control mechanism and partly for fun, you can "freeze" the machine, then ask the participants to slow down to half the "normal" speed or speed up to double-time! Themes can be extremely varied, ranging from lighter subjects such as a football match, fairground and favourite television programmes to topics such as social issues, historical events or scientific concepts. You could have a machine that actually makes something like chocolate biscuits, school dinners or weather conditions.

Small groups can devise their own essence machines on a chosen theme that others try to guess. As pupils become more familiar with the technique they can be encouraged to shape their ideas into a longer sequence of sounds, words and movements.

Examples

Geography

★ The seaside, the town where you live, hot and cold countries, causes of global warming, a busy high street, a railway station.

History

★ Building a Roman town, Victorian child labour, 20th century inventions, famous people and maybe – famous battles!

Literacy

★ A story, an individual character or the world of a play, novel or film.
★ Fairy stories. Nursery rhymes. A Hogwarts machine.

Personal and Social Education

★ Happiness – or any other emotion.

★ Optimism and pessimism machines.

★ The school playground – leading on to exploration of social issues.

Science

★ Electricity, a recycling machine, light and dark (things we associate with light; things we associate with dark), individual colours.

★ A woodland ecosystem with interconnected plants, animals, landscape and weather conditions.

★ A healthy eating machine - and then an unhealthy eating machine.

★ Explore why we need to be green by making a pollution machine!

Miscellaneous

★ Favourite moments from the school outing.

★ Design a quirky machine that makes or does something – writing homework, making the user invisible, manufacturing money from carrots – for other students to guess.

★ Essence machines can quickly create the atmosphere of festivals and special occasions such as Chinese New Year, Diwali, Halloween, Bonfire Night, New Year and Christmas.

See also: *Mime, Soundscape.*

Decision Making Strategies

These two strategies can be used when a character is facing a decision or to encourage students to express their opinions in a physical way.

In this section:

- Conscience Alley

- Where Do You Stand?

Conscience Alley

1 **2** | Whole Class | 15 minutes +

A character walks down an alleyway formed by members of the class as they use persuasive arguments to help make a decision.

Why use it?

Conscience alley (also known as *Decision Alley* and *Thought Tunnel*) can be used to explore any dilemma faced by a character. It encourages pupils to consider a decisive moment in detail by presenting and listening to contrasting opinions and helps to improve vocabulary and reasoning skills.

No, George, don't fight the dragon!

How do you do it?

The class should form two equal lines facing each other, a couple of metres apart. One person (the teacher or a student) takes the role of the character making the decision and slowly walks between the lines, as the "persuaders" whisper or speak their advice. The character can walk straight down the middle or step from side to side as each member of the class offers their viewpoint. If appropriate two or more pupils may walk down the alley together, which can be supportive for younger or less confident children.

Conscience alley is often organised so that those on one side give opposing advice to those on the other. When the character has listened to all the suggestions and reaches the end of the alley he decides on a course of action, weighing up the advice that has been given. Children should be encouraged to come up with reasons of their own – but most importantly each person should try to be persuasive.

Examples

Geography:

★ A town planner consults shopkeepers about whether the high street should be closed to traffic.

★ A tourist weighs up issues of sustainability when deciding where to go on holiday.

★ A developer decides whether to build on a site of scientific interest.

History:

★ The Trojans are deciding whether to bring the wooden horse into the city of Troy.

★ A mother is making up her mind whether to register her children for evacuation from London at the start of World War Two.

★ A farm labourer wonders whether to travel to Manchester to get a job in a cotton mill.

Literacy:

★ Red Riding Hood is deciding whether to speak to the wolf.

★ Tom wonders whether to enter the midnight garden.

★ Romeo is deciding whether to fight Tybalt.

Personal and Social Education:

★ You have seen your best friend cheating in a test. What should you do?

★ You joined in with some bullying and now you feel guilty. What can you do?

★ Your friends steal some toys from a shop while you are with them.

★ Your friends want you to prove how brave you are by walking along a high wall.

Science:

★ A mallard duck is weighing up the pros and cons of building its nest high up in a tree or on the ground.

★ A land developer decides whether to build a nuclear power station or a wind farm.

★ A farmer is deciding whether to allow public access to his land. One side persuades him how he can encourage visitors to respect the countryside and the other side persuades him that the effects of visitors will be too destructive.

See also: *Hot-seating, Role on the Wall, Role Play, Where do you Stand?*

Where Do You Stand?

  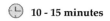 **Whole Class**   🕐 **10 - 15 minutes**

> Students express their views by choosing where to stand on a line representing a continuum of opinion.

Why use it?

Where Do you Stand[7] provides an overall snapshot of everybody's point of view about an issue and enables students to actively demonstrate their opinions in relation to each other. It shows how widely opinions can differ between people and may be used at a moment's notice for reflecting on issues in a drama session or in any subject. The technique can be used before and after exploring a topic to evaluate changes in students' opinions and can easily lead into writing and other activities. It can be used as part of the *Philosophy for Children*[8] approach as well as to review and test learning.

How do you do it?

Position two chairs a good distance apart, representing the two ends of an imaginary line. One chair is "Agree" and the other is "Disagree" (or "yes" and "no" for younger children). You may wish to place a sign on them to show which is which. Read out a statement and ask students to choose a place to stand in relation to the chairs that they feel represents their view. The nearer they stand to one of the chairs, the stronger the opinion they are expressing. Those who don't know, are open-minded or don't want to say can move towards the middle.

Emphasise that everybody's point of view will be respected and encourage children to decide for themselves rather than copy their friends. Give them a few moments to make their decision.

---

[7] Also known as *Spectrum of Difference* (Neelands and Goode 1990).

[8] http://www.philosophy4children.co.uk/

Once everyone has chosen a place, neighbouring students can discuss their decisions with each other. Random pupils from different parts of the continuum can be asked to explain why they have placed themselves at a particular location. After hearing a few comments you can ask if anybody has changed their mind and wishes to move to a new position. It is worth asking pupils to explain why they have moved.

Instead of an imaginary line you can use a length of rope, chalk line or strip of masking tape. The activity can be used in outdoor learning by using two trees or other landmarks.

Examples

Begin by demonstrating the technique with some playful statements:

★ I prefer cats to dogs

★ Chocolate ice-cream is the best flavour

★ Playing a game is more fun than watching television

★ Online games are better than real games

★ Maths is more useful than English

Environmental Studies

★ Precious jewels are more valuable than trees.

★ Recycling helps the rainforests.

★ Land pollution is more serious than air pollution.

★ Building a hydroelectric dam helps sustainability.

★ Eco-tourism is good for developing countries.

Geography

★ Skateboarding should be allowed in the city-centre.

★ All motorised traffic should be banned from city-centres.

★ Clouds are full of rain.

★ There are more people in Scotland than there are in New York.

★ A compass wouldn't work at the North Pole.

History

★ The Industrial Revolution improved Victorian society.

★ The Great Fire of London was a good thing.

ICT

★ Video games help us learn.

★ You can learn more from the internet than you can from books.

★ E-books are better than paper ones.

Literacy

★ Hansel and Gretel were right to run away into the woods.

★ Jack should never have climbed the beanstalk.

Maths

★ A circle has only got one side.

★ If you add two odd numbers together you always get an even number.

★ Triangles always add up to 180 degrees.

★ Three-fifths is bigger than three-quarters.

Personal and Social Education

★ If you break a friend's toy, it's best not to tell them.

★ It's OK to borrow a pencil from a friend without asking.

★ If somebody gives you something that they stole, but they don't tell you it's stolen, then it is OK to keep it.

★ If you find 50p in the street, it's "Finders Keepers" – you are allowed to keep it. What about if you find a wallet?

★ It's never a good idea to take a risk.

★ Homeless people should be allowed to beg on the street.

★ Everyone should be a vegetarian.

★ Cannabis should be legalized.

★ University education should be free.

Science

★   Animals are more important than people.

★   Plants need sunshine more than water.

★   Earthquakes are caused by volcanoes.

★   Testing on animals is essential to scientific progress.

★   Nuclear power is the greenest form of energy.

★   Genetic engineering is essential for scientific progress.

If you are keen to generate further philosophical debate then try *The Little Book of Thunks,* which is full of thought-provoking questions like:

> *Is it ever right to bully a bully?*
>
> *Could a fly cause an aeroplane to crash?*
>
> *Is it ever possible to learn nothing?*

(Gilbert 2007)

Improvisation and Performance

As students develop their confidence, these strategies will provide structures for improvised drama as well as helping them to polish their performance skills.

In this section:

- Improvisation

- Forum Theatre

- Soundscape

- Flashbacks / Flash Forwards

- Ritual

- Marking The Moment

- Living Newspaper

- Whoosh!

- Object Theatre

- Open And Close

- Spotlight

Improvisation 26

Pairs, Groups, Whole Class | 10 minutes +

Improvisation is the spontaneous performance of a scene or story.

Why use it?

Improvisation is already familiar to children as a natural part of play, enabling them to imaginatively explore any situation and its potential outcomes. In educational drama, improvisation develops pupils' confidence, encouraging them to be creative, to cooperate, negotiate, speak and listen. It can be done at any time and requires no lines to be learned. Improvisation can be used to find out more about a story and its characters or to devise new episodes and solutions to problems. This collective story making can be an effective way of motivating children to write. It enables students to share their ideas and views with the group and the rest of the class.

How do you do it?

Improvisation can be done individually, in pairs, groups or as a whole class. It usually involves speech and movement but can be silent. Although it is created spontaneously, improvisation needs some kind of structure – ranging from an opening line to a defined theme or specific situation. Partner work is a good place to start. This could be a conversation on a given theme or an activity enacted together. Once students are clear about the structure, little or no preparation is required.

 Tip:

To establish an improvised situation, try asking the questions "Who?', "What?", "Where?", "When?" and "Why?"

Working in groups requires some initial discussion and negotiation to allocate roles and ensure mutual understanding of the aims. However, pupils should be encouraged to actively try out their ideas. If discussion becomes extended group members may lose interest and become reluctant to begin.

It may not be difficult to start an improvisation but knowing how to finish can be harder. Remind children about stories having a beginning, middle and end – and give them a time limit. The strategy outlined below enables pupils to show their work without falling into this trap.

 Tip:

Moving into improvisation

*Begin with a **still image** created by a group. Use **thought tracking** to find out what each of the characters are thinking and feeling. Explain that you would like the group to bring the scene alive for a few moments with speech and movement. Initiate this by saying "Action!" or clapping your hands to start the scene. Let the improvisation run for a short time – ideally before the performers run out of steam – and then end it with another signal such as "Cut!", "Freeze!" or by clapping your hands a second time. The improvisation does not need to last longer than a minute.*

The group will enjoy being able to tell the story without worrying about how to start or finish the scene and the teacher can easily control how much is shown. After a few sessions of working in this way students will become more confident about devising and presenting short scenes.

Status is used to denote the power relationship between characters in a scene and is a useful way of setting up an improvisation. For example, a master would usually have a high status and a servant would have a low status. However things can get interesting when you reverse the status. A servant with high status has great dramatic potential! Characters can also be of equal status. Usually the status relationship will alter during a scene or improvisation. Start off by playing *Status Images* (see next page).

⚙ Tip:

Status Images

In pairs create a still image where one of you has a higher status than the other, for example a parent telling off a child. Show your image to the others and let them guess who is "high" and who is "low". Sometimes this will be very clear – but not always. Discuss why there may be areas of disagreement. Look at how students have used their body shape, facial expressions, eye-contact, levels and distance from one another. Is one student higher up than the other? Make another image showing high and low status in a different way. Finally try to make an image where you have equal status and see if the onlookers agree!

Examples

Many of the strategies use improvisation. Here are some more ideas.

★ Create an improvisation predicting what will happen next in a story.

★ Devise parallel scenes that could have taken place while the main story was happening.

★ Continue an improvisation from a starting sentence such as *"Haven't I seen you somewhere before?"* or *"Quick, hide, somebody's coming!"*

★ Devise a short TV commercial related to a topic including a jingle and catchphrase, for example *"Come to Ancient Egypt for the holiday of a lifetime."*

★ Tell a fairy tale in a minute.

Further Reading

Hundreds of books have been written about improvisation such as the highly recommended *Impro* (Johnstone 1979). A variety of practical approaches can be found in *101 Drama Games and Activities* (Farmer 2007).

Forum Theatre

  Whole Class  30 minutes +

> Members of the audience are invited to take part in an improvised drama to explore alternative approaches to a problem.

Why use it?

Forum theatre provides an opportunity for members of the audience to explore how a dramatised situation can have alternative outcomes by taking over the role of one or more of the characters. It was originally developed by Augusto Boal as a political tool for change[9] but has been widely adapted for use in educational contexts.

In improvisation it is usually only the actors who perform the drama, but in forum theatre the audience are invited to directly intervene by stopping the action and stepping onto the stage. This means that members of the audience can be on an equal footing with the actors and try out their own ideas for solving problems.

How do you do it?

An improvised play or scene (normally with an unresolved outcome) is shown to the audience all the way through. It is performed a second time and members of the audience – or *spect-actors* as Boal calls them – are invited to stop the action at any point where they think a key character could behave differently. Instead of merely giving verbal suggestions, the spect-actor is invited to demonstrate his or her idea by replacing the character in the scene. In a role that Boal calls the *Joker*, the teacher facilitates communication between the spect-actors and the audience through questioning and discussion.

---

[9] Boal developed forum theatre in his native South America as a way of highlighting political oppression. For further information see *Theatre of the Oppressed* (Boal 1979)

Any member of the audience is allowed to shout "Stop!" At this point the performers pause the scene, the spect-actor comes forward to indicate which character she is replacing and at which point the scene should be re-started. The other actors remain in character, improvising their responses to the alternative behaviour of the new player. They continue until the scene reaches a natural resolution, or until the teacher or a member of the audience stops the action. Different spect-actors may explore several alternatives, choosing where to restart the scene each time, until there is an audience consensus about the best result. Even younger children can take part in a simplified version of forum theatre to explore how characters can behave differently.

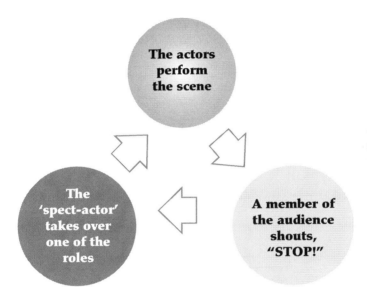

Forum theatre process

Forum theatre can also be used to explore how the quality of a scene may be improved in terms of theatrical presentation. While this is quite different from the original intention of the strategy it helps students experiment with varied approaches to performance and direction. For example if an improvised scene is not working well, instead of just taking suggestions for improvements, you can invite other pupils to demonstrate their ideas.

Fishbowl (Hopkins 2004) is a simple way of exploring the forum theatre approach. Two students role-play a conflict situation with everyone else sitting around them in a circle. The teacher or pupils can freeze the scene at any time to comment or offer advice, which the characters can choose to use or ignore. The action continues from the same point or can be rewound to try a different strategy. This can later be developed with anybody from the circle being invited to step in and take over one of the roles to try out their idea.

Examples

Forum theatre can be used for any story where a character needs to solve a problem, particularly where the obstruction is caused by other characters.

Literacy

★ One of the Billy Goats-Gruff tries out different ways to persuade the Troll to let him cross the bridge.

★ The woodland animals teach the Gruffalo ways of making friends (p.129).

★ Cinderella tries out different ways to avoid being bullied by her stepsisters (p.136).

Personal and Social Education

★ Forum theatre is ideal for exploring social issues such as self-esteem, prejudice, drug abuse, peer pressure, bullying and homelessness[10].

See also: *Flashbacks, Improvisation, Role Play.*

---

[10] The UK theatre company *Cardboard Citizens* uses Forum Theatre to raise awareness about homelessness issues.

Soundscape

28

R 1 2 | 👥 Groups, Whole Class | 🕐 10 minutes +

> Students create the atmosphere of a scene or environment by making appropriate sounds with their bodies and voices. Musical instruments, physical objects and recordings can also be used.

Why use it?

Sound is one of the essential qualities of performance as well as being evocative of people, places and feelings. This technique enables the students to quickly create an atmospheric "sound picture" to help them imagine a particular scene or to provide the live or recorded soundtrack for performance or storytelling. With practice, soundscape can become a very expressive technique.

How do you do it?

Select a theme such as the seaside, a city or a jungle. Sit the pupils in a group and ask them for examples of sounds that might be heard in this environment. Explain that the group is going to create a picture using sound – using their voices (and body percussion if appropriate!) The teacher (or a confident student) acts as conductor whilst the students are the "human orchestra". The conductor controls the overall shape of the soundscape by raising her hand to increase the volume or bringing it to touch the floor for silence. Sections of the group can be faded in and out as appropriate so that all the sounds are heard.

It may be helpful to provide a structure for the soundscape, such as 'a day in the rainforest', 'a storm at sea', or 'a walk through the marketplace' so that the sounds evolve during the piece. You may choose to use simple percussion instruments or everyday objects that make suitable sounds. This works better if you give children an opportunity to explore the sounds they can make with the instruments and to identify which are most appropriate for the soundscape in advance.

In order to have more control over the soundscape, individuals or sections of the orchestra can make different sounds. The sub-groups may rehearse their sounds in advance if necessary. Then the conductor can bring in particular sound textures by gesturing to different sections.

★ Spoken words or phrases can be added to soundscapes to provide atmosphere and to express emotions.

★ If groups are listening to each other's soundscapes, encourage them to close their eyes for a more imaginative experience.

★ Record and play back the soundscape so that students may listen to it critically – they may be pleasantly surprised by the results. This can be used as the soundtrack for an acted or improvised scene.

★ Use mobile phones or digital recorders to collect sounds and play them back as part of a soundscape. Older pupils can edit the found sounds using suitable software such as *Audacity*[11].

---

[11] Available free from www.audacity.sourceforge.net

Examples

Geography

★ Soundscapes lend themselves to representing varied environments and weather conditions.

★ Small groups can create soundscapes for particular countries or locations which the rest of the class have to guess.

★ Groups can create the story of a journey by devising soundscapes for a series of different places.

★ Create the sound of a city with sirens, reversing lorries, spoken conversations, mobile phones, bird song, buskers and market traders.

History

★ Create soundscapes for famous events such as battles – or just an ordinary day in a Victorian city.

★ Make the sounds that might be heard on a journey in the past such as a cart passing through an Iron-age village.

Literacy

★ Develop soundscapes based on pictures in a storybook you are reading. Encourage the children to look carefully at each picture to find as many sounds as they can. Then when you tell the story the children can make the sounds as you show them the picture.

★ In groups tell a story – for example *We're Going on a Bear Hunt* (Rosen 1993) – just using sounds to create the setting, atmosphere, characters and events. Can the other groups guess the story?

★ Give groups a selection of objects like paper cups, water, coins, twigs and stones. Can they make up their own sound story using these?

★ Create a soundscape of a haunted house to lead into poetry or story writing.

★ Create soundscapes of moods such as fear or happiness.

★ Small groups or the whole class can make a collaborative written collage of words spoken during a soundscape (Goodwin 2006, p.34).

Flashbacks / Flash Forwards 29

 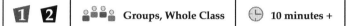 Groups, Whole Class | 10 minutes +

> Participants improvise events that take place before or after a specific moment in time enabling the exploration of characters' motivations and the consequences of their actions.

Why use it?

Adding flashbacks or flash forwards creates a context – it shows what led up to a particular moment, how it might be resolved or how it might develop. The method can be used to quickly bring depth to activities involving still images or improvised drama, helping to flesh out a dramatic moment or create the beginnings of a story.

How do you do it?

With a group that has created a *still image*, explain that when you clap your hands, you would like the students to move silently in slow motion to where their character would have been a few moments before. As they move, they will be watching the other participants, bringing a consensual element to the improvisation. When they are frozen in the new flashback image, you may like to use *thought tracking* to explore character motivation.

If the still image concerns a moment in which there may be heightened dramatic tension, you should explain to participants that any aggressive behaviour would also be slowed down and that there should be no physical contact between individuals.

Now ask them to move back to their original image – which we can call the "present moment". Then you can use flash forwards – participants move in slow motion to indicate where their characters might be a short while later. Using these two techniques you have created an episode with a beginning, middle and end and can develop it in any number of ways. The same approach can be applied by freezing the action in an *improvisation* to enable the creation of new scenes by moving forwards or backwards in time.

Examples

Drama

★   A setting is given, such as a football match, a zoo or a busy street – or a theme is selected, such as bullying or prejudice. The group stands in a circle and one by one, participants step in and make a still image as part of a developing tableau. Nothing is pre-planned. When sufficient characters have been added, thought tracking can be used to establish a little more about the characters, then they *flash back* to a moment just one minute previously. Again they are thought-tracked. They return to the present moment and then *flash forwards* to show what might happen next.

History

★   The technique can be used in a history lesson to show the beginning, middle and end of an important event. Students can photograph the images and add captions or speech bubbles as a way of recording their work.

Ritual 30

 Whole Class | 5 minutes +

> A specially devised sequence of words and movements to mark an important point in a drama.

Why use it?

Rituals can be used to deepen belief in drama or to mark an important moment. They provide an opportunity for all the children to acknowledge one another through a simple group activity. A ritual can provide a way for the whole class to "contract-in" to start and end the drama or to create an opportunity for celebration or reflection within a story. Once learnt, a ritual can be repeated whenever necessary as a way to gather the class together and to reengage in the drama. If you are developing a drama about a particular group, tribe or gang then rituals and ceremonies can become a natural part of the make-believe.

How do you do it?

Rituals can include actions, words, chants, sounds and sung phrases. Encourage children to put forward ideas – a ritual devised using their suggestions is more likely to be remembered.

Examples

★ A ritual can be used to open a meeting or to create a protocol for taking turns to speak.

★ Members of a group in a drama may like to devise their own greeting ceremony.

★ Entering and leaving a make-believe world: Baldwin (2008, p.63) suggests creating a ritual with younger children as a way of starting a whole class drama such as everyone sprinkling "story dust" on their head and repeating special words and actions.

★ In response to a theme the group sits in a circle and each person writes a word or phrase on a card and puts it into a hat, for example words of encouragement for Cinderella.

★ Pupils pass round an empty bag and each person places an imaginary object into it as preparation for a journey (see *Bags and Boxes* *p.59)*.

★ A closing celebration for a topic could include speeches, chants, poetry, human sculptures, artwork and mime.

See also: *Meetings.*

Marking the Moment 31

2 | Groups, Whole Class | ⊕ 15 minutes +

> A drama technique used to highlight a key moment in an improvisation.

Why use it?

Marking the moment enables students to identify and highlight key points within a scene. It can be used to slow down the drama, creating a similar effect to watching a slow-motion scene in a movie or spotlighting an area of the stage during a performance.

How do you do it?

Marking the moment is used after groups have improvised a scene. They should discuss and agree which particular moments they wish to focus on. These can be highlighted through different performance styles or drama strategies. The simplest method is to freeze the action or slow it down but there are many other ways (*see below*). If you have the facilities then music, sound or lighting effects can be added to provide emphasis.

⚛ Tip:

> *Many drama conventions can be used to mark a moment such as:*
>
> *Freeze frames/still images, silence, slow-motion, addressing the audience, spoken or written captions, flashbacks/flash forwards, rewinding the action, mime, music, narration, placards, lighting, sound effects, speaking one word at a time, tableaux, thought tracking and voices in the head. Students are likely to come up with many other creative suggestions.*

The emphasis can be placed on part of a scene – for example in a crowded street the Artful Dodger is teaching Oliver Twist to pick a pocket. The crowd freezes while the two boys move in slow motion. After they have picked the pocket the crowd's movement returns to normal.

Examples

History

The moment when:

★ A slave is taken by the Romans.

★ Sir Walter Raleigh throws down his cloak for Queen Elizabeth.

★ A press gang captures men for the navy.

★ Suffragette Emily Davison throws herself under the King's racehorse.

★ Rosa Parks refuses to give up her bus seat.

Literacy

The moment when:

★ Pandora opens the box and all the evils of the world fly out.

★ The Jabberwock or the Minotaur is slain.

★ The witch locks up Hansel.

★ Grace is given the role of Peter Pan in *Amazing Grace* (Hoffman 2007)

★ The leopard falls down the pit in the *Anansi Stories*.

★ Sherlock Holmes discovers a new clue.

Personal and Social Education

The moment when:

★ A character experiences prejudice.

★ Someone is bullied.

★ Somebody throws litter on the ground.

★ A fire starts in the kitchen.

Living Newspaper $\boxed{32}$

| **2** | 👥 Whole Class | 🕐 60 minutes + |

A thematic approach for linking and presenting a montage of students' work using a range of drama strategies.

Why use it?

A Living Newspaper[12] encourages pupils to discuss, edit and communicate ideas and information. Different aspects of a theme and varying viewpoints can easily be presented. The process can be used to develop a performance (e.g. for the school assembly) or as a plenary/reviewing technique. A Living Newspaper contains factual content similar to that of a newspaper or television documentary except that the medium is drama. Living Newspapers are best used with pupils who are able to develop work in groups and are familiar with a range of drama strategies.

How do you do it?

Explain that the class are going to produce a living newspaper that will be seen and heard rather than read. Show them an ordinary newspaper and ask them to identify the various sections and features that could be used. Divide students into groups and assign them particular topics or pages to create. You may wish to nominate an editor or editorial team for groups to submit their ideas to.

Groups should choose headlines, which can be narrated or perhaps spoken *one word at a time* around the group. Students should be encouraged to find their own novel way of doing this. They should decide on key points to show in their presentation and how to present their material. If they need interviews or photographs, how can they show these? Encourage

---

[12] Living Newspapers, here adapted for classroom use, were developed in the USA during the 1930's to raise awareness of human rights issues, although their roots can be traced back to the Russian Revolution.

London, March 20   SPECIAL EDITION   5 PENCE

TASTY LOAF BAKERY
Pudding Lane
LONDON

CROMWELL
BASHES CAVALIERS!!

pupils to dramatise their material as much as possible rather than rely on pure narration. Older students can decide what kind of slant to present – for example that of a broadsheet or the popular press. Interest can be added by including updates or special reports about breaking news.

Many drama strategies lend themselves to this approach. *Still images* and *tableaux* can be used for photos, *hot seating* for interviews, *flashbacks* and *flash forwards* for comic strips, *narration* for parts of articles as well as *mime* and improvised scenes. The project may need to be developed over several lessons. If there is time to polish your presentation, then you could consider adding music, props, costumes and visual artwork such as posters or projections – as well as videoing the whole project.

⊛ Tip:

Your living newspaper can include headlines, reports, feature articles, interviews and letters as well as photographs (using still images), a weather forecast, horoscopes, cartoons, comic strips, sport reports, book reviews, an agony aunt page, advertisements and quizzes.

Examples

Current Affairs

★ Students make a living newspaper about events that concern them, locally or worldwide, such as human rights or environmental issues.

History

★ A living newspaper set in the seventeenth century could include extracts from Pepys' diary, improvised scenes of the Plague and the Great Fire of London, reports about the royal family, comic strips about the English Civil War and a letter from Oliver Cromwell to the agony aunt.

Geography

★ News, reports and views from another country or the local area.

Literacy

★ Base your newspaper on a fictional story with hot seating or interviews that include the perspectives of central and minor characters. Students can devise *still images* for the cover and illustrations, as well as performing extracts of the story. You could take photos of the performances and add writing and other artwork to make an actual newspaper for display or publication.

Plenary

★ Pairs or small groups can develop presentations summarising aspects of a lesson or highlights of the week including human-interest stories and lessons learned.

Science

★ Groups can present the latest discoveries from science classes in several different ways, for example as a scientific journal, a popular magazine and a comic strip.

See also: *Flashbacks, Hot Seating, Improvisation, Still Images, Mime, Narration, Storytelling, Tableaux.*

Whoosh! 33

1 **2** | 👥 **Whole Class** | 🕐 **10 minutes +**

> A quick and interactive way of teaching a story plot to children of all ages – in a way they will remember!

Why use it?

Whoosh![13] is an engaging and interactive storytelling technique which enables any story to be brought alive quickly even without prior knowledge of the characters or plot. It provides a great way of introducing children to Shakespeare and other complex stories as well as acting out ones they already know. Students will listen to, take part in and most of all remember the story because they help to tell it.

---

[13] 'Whoosh!' was devised by Dr Joe Winston of The University of Warwick and is regularly used by the Royal Shakespeare Company.

In addition to being the storyteller, the teacher has a guiding role a bit like an orchestral conductor crossed with a theatre director. As well as playing characters, pupils become objects, places or events such as a window, a church, a ship, the sun or a storm.

How do you do it?

The whole class stands or sits in a circle. Explain that everybody will have the chance to participate in the telling of a story by becoming the characters and objects. All they have to do is step into the space and make a still image. Sometimes they will have actions to do or words to speak. If at any time you say "Whoosh!" and wave your arms, they should quickly return to their places. Begin the narrative and as soon as a key character, event or object is mentioned, indicate the first student to step into the circle to make a shape or pose. If two or more characters are introduced they can step in at the same time. If necessary several people can take part at once – for example as a forest.

As more characters or objects are introduced, pick students from all around the circle so that everybody can take part. This means that different pupils get to play the same character at various times and everyone gets a chance at trying several roles regardless of gender. The story continues to be told with more students stepping in as required so that a scene is quickly built up. Pupils can interact with one another and speak improvised dialogue or lines from a play. This can be done with you reading the line and the character repeating it.

Any time that the activity inside the circle becomes too lively, congested or confused, simply wave your arms, say "Whoosh!" and everyone returns to their original places to become members of the audience again. It's like wiping the slate clean. The story continues to be told with characters stepping into the space as required. You can say "Whoosh!" as many times as necessary during the story – it's a very useful secret weapon!

You can simply use an existing story and tell it from memory or read it from the book, although it is obviously helpful if you can watch what is going on. If the story is more complex, you may need to use a plot summary along with extracts of the text. As students become more confident with this approach they can take responsibility for stepping into the circle without you needing to tell them. You don't really need any materials as people pretending to be objects is limitless and very entertaining. However adding a few props to play with can be a great way of creating spontaneous ideas for rehearsal.

Examples

You don't have to stick with Shakespeare – almost any story can be used with Whoosh! – including fairy tales, traditional stories from different cultures (such as *Tales of Anansi* or the *Arabian Nights*), narrative poetry and accounts of historical and religious events. You can use the technique to tell the whole or just part of a story; if it is particularly long it can be divided into episodes. Synopses of Shakespeare's plays can be found at www.shakespeare-literature.com and www.rsc.org.uk. The *RSC Shakespeare Toolkit for Teachers* (2010 pp. 172, 221) has ready-made summaries of *A Midsummer Night's Dream* and *Romeo and Juliet* with key characters and objects marked in bold for use with Whoosh!

Here is an example of a story which I used with a mixed group of reception and Year 5 pupils on a *Creative Partnerships* project to introduce *Theseus and the Minotaur*[14]. The words in capitals indicate where you can ask pupils to step forward; the parts they play range from islands and fish to kings and a monster. Before narrating the story I rehearsed a storm **soundscape** with the children. We had also practiced making a labyrinth by holding hands to make a maze shape.

> *There is a beautiful part of the world, called Greece. The SUN shines for nearly all the year, smiling at all the people. Greece has LOTS OF ISLANDS surrounding it – all different shapes and sizes. The biggest of these islands is called CRETE. Many years ago, on that island lived KING MINOS. He was very scary. If he walked through the street, everybody would rush out of his way just in case he got annoyed with them. WHOOSH!*
>
> *Being an island, Crete was surrounded by the sea, with lots of FISHES swimming through it. And in the sea lived one of the gods – POSEIDON! He carried a TRIDENT – like a huge fork with three prongs. He controlled the waves and could bring stormy weather just by banging his trident on the ground. (Conduct STORM Soundscape.) WHOOSH!*
>
> *KING MINOS had a beautiful wife called PASIPHAE. And they had several happy CHILDREN – who played together all day. One day Pasiphae had a new BABY. She showed it to King Minos. But it had a bull's head and a boy's body! King Minos let the child grow up although he was very ashamed. WHOOSH!*

---

[14] Thanks to artist Fiona Muller who developed the project with myself and the staff and children of Mile Cross Primary School, Norwich.

So KING MINOS decided to build a LABYRINTH (several children holding hands) - *a huge maze with lots of corridors and tunnels. And he put the MINOTAUR in the middle of it! The Minotaur kept getting lost in the labyrinth. He was very lonely – and hungry. WHOOSH!*

On the mainland of Greece lived KING AEGEUS. Like most people he was a bit scared of King Minos. One year they held the Olympics, where SPORTSMEN AND WOMEN competed in different events. King Minos's son ANDROGEUS won all the prizes in every competition he entered. Some of the Greek people were so cross that they killed him (encourage Androgeus to mime death). *WHOOSH!*

So KING MINOS declared war on Greece and he won. He said that every nine years SEVEN YOUTHS and SEVEN MAIDENS had to be sent over to Crete on a SHIP to be fed to the Minotaur! The weather was stormy and the sea was rough but POSEIDON let the ship pass by. WHOOSH!

Now KING AEGEUS had a son called THESEUS. He was a hero, brave and strong – and good at wrestling giant turtles. He told his Dad "I will go to Crete", (child repeats line) "I will wrestle the Minotaur to the ground - or die!" (Child repeats line). WHOOSH!

The story can be continued in this way or by using other drama strategies such as *storytelling, improvisation* and *still images*. All the pupils enjoyed taking part in this dramatic storytelling, regardless of age. It led on to a project where we used further drama, music and art activities to explore different aspects of the story.

See also: *Helicopter Technique, Improvisation, Narration, Storytelling.*

Object Theatre  34

| R | 1 | 2 | | ⚇ Groups | | 🕐 15 minutes + |

> Everyday objects are brought to life through simple puppetry.

Why use it?

Endowing objects with characteristics or turning them into something else is a natural part of children's symbolic play from an early age. Puppets fascinate children and this activity provides a simple way for them to create their own characters, invent stories and talk to each other in role.

How do you do it?

Just showing children a collection of interesting objects will soon engage them if you explain that you want them to create characters and make up stories. Encourage them to play with one object for a while, moving it around in different ways to see how many different things it can be. It won't take long before some of the objects start to "come to life" and children can be encouraged to explore whether the object could be some kind of creature. Soon the object creatures will be ready to interact with and "talk" to each other (with pupils providing improvised dialogue).

It may be possible to attach objects to each other or hold them together and move them around as one character. For example, a piece of string can provide legs for a banana or hair for an orange. It is surprising how quickly an object can seem to have a character of its own. Stick on "googly" eyes can be ordered cheaply from craft suppliers to quickly add personality to object creatures.

We often see objects come to life in filmed animations but you can create your own live animations through simple puppetry. Videoing the children's object characters interacting with one another can make for quite an entertaining show. Pupils can also paint scenery for the backdrop as well as write their own play scripts or adaptations of stories.

 Tip:

Useful Objects

Most objects can become something else with a dash of imagination, but here are a few ideas to get you started: tea strainer, cup, jug, rubber glove, bits of string and rope, scraps of fabric, traditional hand fan, funnel, whisk, paintbrush, hairbrush, toothbrush, comb, plastic bottle, fruit and vegetables, wooden spoon, salt and pepper pots.

See Also: *Bags and Boxes, Narration, Speaking Objects, Storytelling, Ten Second Objects.*

Open and Close

35

1 **2** | 👥 Groups | 🕐 15 minutes +

> A technique for telling a story through a series of still images, where the audience open and close their eyes to keep each image clear and separate in their minds.

Why use it?

This simple and effective technique mimics the effect of blackouts on stage or frames in a comic strip – with no technical equipment required. The strategy develops narrative skills as well as group negotiation and cooperation. It can be used to actively test comprehension of a narrative or series of events. The process enables the group and the audience to focus on the important images rather than the movement between them. The result is surprisingly effective and has to be seen to be believed!

How do you do it?

Divide the class into small groups and give them the task of telling a story using a specific number of still images – three is a good number as they need to remember them all. Once they have worked out their key images they should practice moving from one to the next. When the time comes for sharing the work, the teacher (or a member of the group) should take responsibility for saying "Open" and "Close".

The audience should close their eyes while the group gets into position. When the group has its first image ready, the designated person says "Open". The audience open their eyes for a few moments and look carefully at the scene. When they have had time to take everything in, the same person says, "Close" and the audience close their eyes again. The group moves quickly and quietly into the second position and then the audience are asked to open their eyes. The process is repeated until all the images have been shown. The effect is similar to looking at a series of photographs or a three-dimensional cartoon strip.

Examples

★ Use the technique as a way of helping a group to create their own story for creative writing.

★ Students can take photographs of the group images to make their own cartoon strip. All they need to do is add the speech bubbles.

★ You can set a theme like well-known movies, stories from history or scientific discoveries, with each group secretly choosing their own story. Then the audience has to guess what it was.

★ Set each group a different section of a story to create, then you can show them in the correct order to retell the story.

★ Review understanding of a topic by asking students to summarise their learning through a sequence of images.

★ For extra dramatic effect play some atmospheric music while groups show their images. Silent movie music would be good for a sequence based on the Victorians.

★ If you are planning to turn a story into a play, this is a great way of getting groups to generate ideas which you can embellish for performance.

See also: *Flashbacks, Improvisation, Spotlight, Still Images, Storytelling, Tableaux, Whoosh!*

Spotlight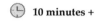

  Groups | 10 minutes +

> Spotlighting is a technique for enabling small groups to share their improvisational work.

Why use it?

When students show improvised drama it is naturally difficult for them to know when and how to finish. As the scene dissolves into confusion, other groups may be wondering when they will have their turn rather than paying attention to the performance. This strategy solves both problems. The teacher controls the time taken by each group and the order in which they perform. Just like a real spotlight, the technique focuses the attention on one area of the room at a time and makes it clear as to which group is taking its turn.

How do you do it?

When all the groups are ready to show their improvisations, ask them to sit on the floor. Explain that you will walk around the room and as you get close to each group, that group will stand up and show part of their improvisation. As you move off towards the next group they will stop the drama and quietly sit down again so that they can watch other groups.

As you stand near to each group you can judge when the improvisation is about to run out of steam or when you and the class have seen enough. This could be anything from ten seconds to a minute or more. The students all know that they have a chance to share their work without worrying about how and when to stop the scene.

See also: *Improvisation, Open and Close, Storytelling.*

Drama Lessons

Once you have explored the use of drama strategies in subject areas you will be ready to apply them to a developed theme. The drama lessons are designed as versatile frameworks – you can work through all the activities or use them according to need. The approaches can easily be adapted for other topics and age-groups.

In this section:

The Gruffalo
Using drama to explore and extend a story

Listen To Me
Constructive approaches to bullying behaviour

Away From Home
Exploring what it was like for children evacuated during World War II

The Gruffalo

  Ages 4–7 years

A variety of approaches for using drama strategies to support and extend learning through *The Gruffalo* (Donaldson 1996).

Illustration from *The Gruffalo Pop-Up Theatre Book* (Donaldson 2008)

Strategies used: Conscience Alley, Forum Theatre, Hot Seating, Role Play, Still Images, Teacher in Role, Soundscape.

Learning Objectives for Drama:

In this unit students will:

★ Use language to imagine and recreate roles and experiences

★ Explore familiar themes and characters through improvisation and role play

★ Act out a well-known story using voices for characters

★ Present part of the story for members of the class

Drama Activities

Meet a Creature

Drama strategies can easily be introduced as a way of enhancing a storytelling session. Begin by reading the first part of *The Gruffalo* to the children up until the end of the first meeting with the fox. Show them the pictures and discuss the story with them as usual. Now you are going to introduce the techniques of *teacher in role (p.20)* and *hot seating (p.28)*. No acting skills are required; you simply talk to the students as if you were a character. This is only a small step from reading the story aloud. The techniques can help the children examine and discuss the feelings of the characters.

Show the children the double page spread before the title page and ask them what creatures they can see there (a butterfly, a beetle and a woodpecker.) Ask them what questions they would put to any of these characters if they met them about what has happened in the story. Explain that you are going to pretend to be one of these creatures and that you will show when you are pretending to be the character by putting on a special hat (or other piece of token costume). You can choose which of the three creatures to be. Step away from your chair and put on the hat (a baseball cap might suit the woodpecker). Sit down again and begin by saying "hello" as the character.

You can give the children clues about who you are by telling them where you live and what you have noticed. Encourage them to find out who you are and to pose questions about what you have seen. Ask pupils questions too. In this way you can encourage the children to recap on the story so far by questioning them about why the fox ran away. It's up to you how much detail you ask for. You can finish by quoting the mouse's words:

> *Silly old Fox! Doesn't he know,*
> *There's no such thing as a Gruffalo?*

Then simply say goodbye and remove the hat to signify that you are stepping out of role. You can repeat this at other points in the story, taking different roles such as the fox, the owl, the snake and the mouse. It is useful to decide what kind of issues each of the characters can raise:

Meet the Mouse

Themes: *Being scared/being brave. Telling lies.*

Attitude: *I know I acted bravely, but really I'm quite scared. Are you ever scared of anything? Yes, I told lies – because I was scared. Was it wrong to tell lies? What else could I have done? Anyway it turned out to be true because there was a Gruffalo.*

Meet the Owl

Themes: *Trust. Being scared. Food chains.*

Attitude: *I'm sure you know that I only wanted to invite the mouse for tea in my treetop house. Wouldn't you like to come for tea with me as well? I admit that I might have wanted to eat the mouse but I've got to eat something – what do you think us owls eat? I'll tell you something though – I'm not sure if that mouse was telling the truth. But I'm not going to hang around to find out.*

Once you have demonstrated this a few times then individual children can also be hot-seated as story characters while the rest of the class ask them questions. They can also do this in pairs or small groups.

Sounds of the Forest

Create a *soundscape (p.101)* of the forest using vocal sounds and/or simple percussion instruments.

Exploring the Woods

Ask the children to travel around the space as different animals moving through the forest. As well as the main characters – the mouse, fox, owl and snake – there are others that appear in drawings including a frog, butterfly, beetle, woodpecker, kingfisher, dragonfly, squirrel and snail (the Gruffalo can come later). You can play recorded music or forest sound effects or simply shake a tambourine to signal when the pupils should move.

The children can also make shapes of different objects in the forest such as trees, plants, fallen logs, stones or streams using *still images (p.63)*. You can use this as an opportunity to explore different levels – high, medium and low – as well as positional language. Then half the class can make the forest shapes while the others move amongst them as animals. They should decide what their animal is doing – looking for food or making a home, for example. Stop and ask the students what they would do if they heard the Gruffalo coming. Would they lie down, stand still or hide in different parts of the woods? When the Gruffalo has gone they can check to see if the coast is clear and then carry on with their activities. Explain that you will bang a tambourine to make the sound of the Gruffalo's footsteps getting louder. Try this a couple of times and let everyone have a go at being animals reacting to the Gruffalo.

As a development you can combine the activities with one group making the forest shapes, another making a soundscape and the third group moving through the forest as animals. The sounds and movement can stop when the Gruffalo appears. You can also use this as an opportunity to explore the topics of animal homes and ecosystems.

Story Moments

Pupils can create still images of key moments from the story – sad moments, happy moments, scary moments – for example the occasion when the Gruffalo and the mouse first meet. If this is during the story reading, then the children can make a second frozen picture to show what they think happens next. The following activities can be used when they have heard the whole story.

Funny Faces

Explore facial expressions of characters at various points in the story. Invite the children to stand in a circle. Explain that they are going to use their faces to show how characters felt at different times in the story. Choose a character and a moment, for example the fox when he first met the mouse. Count down *Three-Two-One* and clap your hands or shake a tambourine as a signal for them to make the face. You can pick out some of the expressions to show the others. How would they describe the feelings being shown on other pupils' faces? Then choose a different moment/animal, for example the fox when he sees the Gruffalo.

Gruffalo's Footsteps

Ask the children how well the animals know the Gruffalo – probably not very well at all. In this adaptation of *Grandma's Footsteps* they will attempt to creep up to the Gruffalo without being seen. The **teacher in role** (or teaching assistant) as the Gruffalo stands at one end of the space (you can also play this outside on the field or in the woods) and the children stand behind a line. Again, you can use some token costume such as a hat or shawl to denote that you are in role. The students have to move as woodland animals towards you whenever you are not looking. If they are completely still the Gruffalo will not see them. Turn your back on them and look around periodically. Anyone who moves when you are looking has to go back to the start. Before too long one of them will get close enough to tap you on the shoulder. It is likely the children will want to play this several times with different pupils taking it in turns to be the Gruffalo.

Meet the Gruffalo

Now that they have managed to creep up on the Gruffalo, it is time for the animals to meet him through teacher in role. This is an opportunity for them to think about the character of the Gruffalo and how he may be feeling. While he is a fierce animal, he may slowly reveal that he has a softer side. The children can be in role as animals from the forest.

Themes: *Friendship, looking different.*

Attitude: *This is my forest and if I want to eat anyone I will – but I'm not hungry at the moment. Who are you lot and what do you want? Why are you looking at me like that? I can't help the way I look. Do you think I look strange? I quite like having a wart on the end of my nose and I'm very proud of my tusks. They give me character. The only problem is, I don't know any other Gruffaloes. Any time I want to play a game, other animals just run away. What do you think I can do to try and make friends with the animals?*

Be open to the children's suggestions. You can ask them to show you how they make friends and they could demonstrate some of these strategies, such as shaking hands, offering to play games and so on. Whether they do that with you will depend on how fierce you're feeling! This could lead onto other activities such as making gifts for the Gruffalo or writing letters to him. These could be "posted" in a suitable place if you have access to nearby trees, for example in a hollow or under a rock.

How to Make Friends

Ask the children how you should behave when you meet other animals and what you can do to appear more friendly. Invite some of them to meet you in role as an animal. At first you can behave somewhat insensitively – growling or asking them if you look fierce. Encourage them to try different ways of helping you to be friendlier such as teaching you how to smile without showing your scary fangs for example. When they have got the hang of this you can ask one of the children to take over your role as the Gruffalo. Now you can use a simplified form of *forum theatre* (p.98) where children try out different ways of making friends. Pupils in the audience can say "Stop!" whenever they think something isn't working. Whoever says "Stop" can come forward and try out a new idea. This should generate a lot of ideas about making friends.

Advice Line

Explain that the Gruffalo needs advice about making friends and the children are going to give him some help using *conscience alley (p.87)*. The pupils form two lines and a member of staff walks in between them in the role of the Gruffalo. The children whisper advice as the Gruffalo moves past them. It can also be fun to combine this with the forest exercise, using *speaking objects (p.76)*. When the children have made the forest using still images, the teacher moves through the forest in role as the Gruffalo. As she passes by each object or animal the child whispers their suggestion.

Other Characters

As well as exploring the viewpoints of the story characters, teacher in role can be used to consider peripheral characters such as the Mouse's mother.

Mouse's mother

Theme: *Stranger danger.*

Attitude: *Has anyone seen my son/daughter? She went out to play this morning but I haven't seen her for ages. I told her to be careful who she talks to. Do you know where she is? She was talking to a what? A Gruffalo?*

This could lead to you asking for ideas of how to find the mouse and further improvisation e.g. an animal search party or artwork such as "Lost" and "Wanted" posters.

Plenary

After you have used some of these approaches be sure to discuss any issues raised with the children *out of role* to ensure they make connections between the make-believe and their own lives.

Listen to Me

1 **2** | Ages 5–11 years |

A series of drama and writing activities exploring bullying issues through the story of Cinderella.

Strategies used: Essence Machines, Forum Theatre, Improvisation, Tableaux, Teacher in Role, Ten Second Objects, Role Play, Rumours, Speaking Objects, Thought Tracking, Whoosh!

Learning Objectives for Drama

In this unit students will:

★ Use a range of drama strategies to explore social issues

★ Engage and empathise with characters and situations from a known story through drama

★ Use vocal and physical expression to communicate emotions and behaviour

★ Communicate ideas through performance

★ Work together in groups to share ideas

★ Present the viewpoints of different characters through dialogue, role-play and writing

★ Identify and discuss the qualities of others' performances

Introduction

This unit outlines a series of activities that can be used as a framework for exploring bullying issues through the story of Cinderella. The content can be adjusted according to the age-range and needs of the group and be developed over a series of sessions. The approach is based on the *Restorative Justice* model focusing on how an individual's behaviour affects others and how they may learn from it. Restorative practice can easily be incorporated as part of a whole-school approach to dealing with conflict.

> *One of the outcomes of restorative practice is that children come to understand the harm they can do to others so that they make better choices in the future.*
>
> (Thorsborne and Vinegrad 2009)

Drama Activities

Story Objects

To introduce the topic, play *ten second objects (p.73)*. Divide the children into groups of around five pupils and call out the names of objects from the story. They have ten seconds to form each object out of themselves. Examples could include a fireplace, a pumpkin, a coach and two horses, a broom, a glass slipper and a palace.

Story Moments

Explain that the children are going to explore how Cinderella's stepsisters bullied her and whether the characters could learn to behave differently. As an introductory activity you can begin with an *essence machine (p.82)* based on the story. The class makes a circle and anyone can start by stepping forward and making a repeating sound (or words) and movement. For example, one person might step forward as the Fairy Godmother and wave an imaginary magic wand, saying, "You shall go to the ball!" Another might mime Cinderella cleaning the floor (with suitable sounds) and two other children could step in as Cinderella dancing with the prince or the clock striking midnight. Each person repeats their sound and action until as many children as wish to have stepped in. After a while you can stop the action with "Freeze!" and ask everyone to rejoin the circle. The class will have generated many layers of images, sounds and phrases from the story.

As an alternative introduction you can play **Whoosh!** *(p.114)* using a suitable version of the story.

Meet Cinderella

Explain that you are going to pretend to be a different character for a while and that you want the students to help you. As **teacher in role** *(p.20)* you will play Cinderella – but you don't need to specify the character, as they will soon work it out. Put on a simple piece of costume (such as an apron) to designate when you are in role. A duster in the pocket is a useful addition. Your aim is to present Cinderella's point of view, highlighting how she is treated and how it makes her feel. Take out the duster, start a menial task such as cleaning the floor and then begin talking to the children along the following lines:

> *They always make me do this. I don't mind helping around the house but it would be nice if somebody said "Thanks" once in a while. Most of the time I just get ignored. When they do notice me they just call me names. In fact they're really rude to me. You know who I'm talking about, don't you? My stepsisters. They always think they're better than me. They don't include me in their games or their dressing up. They've got such lovely clothes and shoes. All I've got are these rags. They're filthy because I just have to clean the house all the time. I wish I could have nice things like them. Well, at least I can dream. Do you ever have to do dirty jobs at home? Do you like it? I don't, not when I have to do it all the time. I'd better go, because I think I can hear them coming to check up on me.*

Now come out of character and ask the class who they met. What did they find out about Cinderella? How did her stepsisters treat her? This leads on to the following activity.

Bullying Images

Ask the class for examples of ways that Cinderella's stepsisters were hurtful towards her in the story such as:

★   Forcing Cinderella to do the housework

★   Calling her names

★   Ignoring her

★   Teasing her

★   Hiding the invitation to the ball

★   Taunting her when she asks to try on the slipper

⊕ Tip:

Types of Bullying include:

Direct bullying such as verbal, physical, threats, gestures, extortion and cyber-bullying.

Indirect bullying such as exclusion, ignoring, spreading rumours and writing notes or sending texts.

Discuss the different kinds of bullying that take place in the story. Explain that you would like students to work in small groups to create *tableaux (p.67)* of some of these moments – as well as others that they think could have taken place (with younger or less experienced children these can be created with the whole class in a circle). How else might the sisters have bullied Cinderella? Ask students to think about other examples of bullying that they might know about. After a minute or two ask groups to share their work.

Other ideas they come up with could include:

★   Making Cinderella do the stepsisters' school homework

★   Gossiping behind her back

★ Stealing her belongings

★ Threatening her

Discuss the different ideas presented by each group and how they showed them. Were they clear images? How did students use their bodies and facial expression to communicate what was happening? *Thought tracking (p.31)* can also be used to explore the content of the images.

Bring the Images to Life

Some groups can bring their scenes to life through *improvisation (p.95)* using action and words. You can demonstrate with one of the groups how slow motion *mime* can be used to show physical bullying with no bodily contact. As the scenes and images are presented you can draw out discussion relating to the different types of bullying.

Spreading Rumours

In this activity you will look at how *rumours (p.39)* about people can spread and develop through indirect verbal bullying. The children should think about what the stepsisters might say about Cinderella. They should spread out in the space and start to walk around, mixing and mingling. When they have an idea about what one of the stepsisters might say they can whisper it to somebody else, for example *"I've heard that Cinderella is really lazy"*. They should listen to the other rumours that people tell them and pass these on, adding to them if they wish. After a couple of minutes call them together and ask them to share what they heard. How did the rumours develop? Do they think any of the rumours were true? How did they feel when they passed on the rumours? Why would the sisters have said these things about Cinderella?

Speaking Objects *(p.76)*

Gather students into a large circle. Explain that in this activity they are going to make the shapes of objects that would be found in Cinderella's house. These can include pieces of furniture or items belonging to her or her stepsisters. When anybody has an idea they can step into the circle and make the shape stating what they are, for example "I am the grandfather clock", or "We are the fireplace."

Explain that in a moment Cinderella's Fairy Godmother is going to enter the house and walk around it. Because she is "magic", the objects can talk to her and tell her what they have seen happening. Enter the circle in role and ask the objects questions focussing on how Cinderella has been bullied and what they have seen. You could even wave a magic wand at the objects when you want them to speak.

Forum Theatre *(p.98)*

In this section groups will plan and improvise a scene showing Cinderella being bullied that should last no longer than one or two minutes. You can allocate ideas the class generated earlier so that each group works on a different type of bullying. Students can be asked to use slow-motion movement to show any bullying that may have a physical element. The idea at this point is not to find a happy ending but just to demonstrate how the bullying occurred.

Allow the students ten to fifteen minutes to develop their scenes. When they have shown the pieces, select one where the performers seem confident and the situation is unresolved. Ask the audience if they can think of other ways Cinderella could have behaved in this scene to bring a different outcome. Would one of them like to try out their idea by stepping into the scene to take over the role of Cinderella? Replay the scene to allow them to do this. The other performers should react to the new Cinderella as they think their character would – don't let them make it too easy for her. In this way you can allow different children to try out various strategies. You can use the same approach to explore other groups' scenes as appropriate.

Older students can be encouraged to look at how characters use body language and eye contact successfully and unsuccessfully. Which characters were really listening to each other's ideas? If appropriate, additional characters can be introduced such as Cinderella's father or stepmother. However, avoid a "magic" solution – the strategies should be transferable to the real world. It may be that some of the situations cannot be satisfactorily resolved until the sisters learn that they can change their behaviour.

Discuss with the children which strategies were most successful. If there are further suggestions these can also be tried.

Learning to Listen

In this section *hot seating (p.28)* is used to question the feelings, attitudes and behaviour of Cinderella and her stepsisters after the bullying has taken place. The questioning approach is based on the 'restorative chat' outlined in *'Restorative Justice Pocketbook'* (Thorsborne and Vinegrad 2009). This aims to encourage characters to assess their behaviour, to think about how it has affected others and to work out a way of putting things right.

a) Explain that you are going to try and find out why the **stepsisters** behaved as they did. This activity uses *collective role (p.18)* to enable the whole class to share and support each other's ideas: all the students will take on the role of the stepsisters simultaneously so that any one of them may take a turn to speak in character. It is important that children listen to each other's contributions.

Explain that the stepsisters are not in trouble – you just want to talk about what happened rather than be judgmental. Instead of using 'why?' questions ask them about specific things they did, such as:

★ What were you thinking when you called Cinderella names?

★ What was going on in your mind when you stole her money?

★ What did you hope would happen when you made a rude face at her?

★ What do you think it was like for Cinderella when you did these things?

★ How do you think it affected her?

b) Explain that the class are going to meet **Cinderella** again to find out how she was affected by what the stepsisters did. In this activity one student at a time takes on the role of Cinderella. For continuity they can wear the same apron or other costume that you used as teacher in role. Guide the class in asking Cinderella about issues previously raised with the stepsisters:

★ What did you think when the stepsisters called you names?

★ What was it like for you?

★ What was the worst thing about having your money stolen?

★ What did you think and feel when the sisters treated you like that?

★ What do you think about what the stepsisters told us when we talked to them just now?

After a while you can swop over to allow other students an opportunity to play the role.

Finding Resolution

Discuss with the class how they think the stepsisters might react if they heard Cinderella talking just now. In small groups they should plan and rehearse a devised scene where Cinderella tells the stepsisters how she feels about what they did. What might the stepsisters think about that and what would they say to Cinderella now? What could they do to try and make things better? (This could include an apology.)

Show some scenes and discuss how convincing they were. Do the students think Cinderella would have been happy with the promises that were made in the scenes? You can also use more *forum theatre* if you wish.

Discussion

Class discussion provides an opportunity to link these issues to the students' own experience. In a circle, discuss with the pupils what they have learnt about bullying, its effect on those who are bullied and whether it is possible to make things better. This could lead onto advice about what children should do if they think they are being bullied. This should be linked to the school's Anti-Bullying policy and might include some of the suggestions below:

★ Tell someone you trust such as an adult or friend

★ Be respectful to each other

★ Be supportive to someone who is bullied

★ Avoid the situation if possible

★ Try to stay calm

Where Do You Stand? *(p.90)*

This activity enables pupils to express their opinions and sums up what they have learnt. Set up two chairs with "Agree" and "Disagree" signs.

Read out one statement at a time and ask the children to place themselves according to what they believe, stressing that there is not always a "right" answer. Pupils standing near each other can discuss their decisions and random students can be picked out to explain why they have chosen their particular location. Following this, children can change position if they have formed a new opinion.

Suitable statements include:

★ *It's best to keep it a secret if you are bullied.*

★ *If you see somebody in trouble you should try to stop the bullies.*

★ *It's OK to call someone a name if you are only joking.*

★ *It's better to tell a friend about bullying than to tell the teacher.*

★ *If you ignore bullies they will go away.*

★ *Anyone can be a bully.*

Writing

The drama work can easily develop into writing. Here are a few suggestions:

★ Pin the apron that was used for Cinderella to the wall. Over a few days students can write notes or letters giving advice to Cinderella and leave them in the apron pocket. These can be read out later.

★ Do the same for the stepsisters, using appropriate props or paintings of them with each holding a bag into which notes can be placed.

★ Write an entry in Cinderella's diary about a time that she was bullied, how she felt and what she thinks she can do about it.

★ In pairs or groups write a script of a meeting between two of the characters in the story. Act it out.

★ Write letters from the stepsisters to Cinderella explaining how they feel now and how they plan to behave in the future.

★ Design anti-bullying posters based on the story to display around the school.

Resources

http://www.restorativejustice.org.uk

Away From Home: Evacuees

 Ages 7–11 years

Drama and writing activities exploring the experiences of children evacuated during the Second World War.

Strategies used: Conscience Alley, Hot Seating, Role on the Wall, Role Play, Rumours, Speaking Objects, Spotlight, Tableaux, Teacher in Role, Thought Tracking.

Learning Objectives for Drama

In this unit students will:

★ Use a range of drama strategies to explore social issues

★ Engage and empathise with characters and situations from a story

★ Use vocal and physical expression to communicate emotions and behaviour

★ Communicate ideas through performance

★ Work together in groups to share ideas

★ Present the viewpoints of different characters through dialogue, role-play and writing

★ Identify and discuss the qualities of others' performances

Introduction

The unit uses a range of media, drama strategies and a fictional story to explore the experience of World War Two evacuees. Extensive resources about the topic are readily available in the form of history books, children's fiction, films, museums and websites. A wide range of verbatim accounts is available from the BBC WW2 People's War website and archive radio recordings can be streamed from BBC School Radio or ordered on CD along with transcripts of the recordings. Links to external websites and a list of resources are given at the end of the unit. The material can be extended over several sessions. The links can also be found at www. LearningThroughDrama.com.

Drama Activities

Packing a Suitcase

With the class standing in a circle explain that one and a half million children, teachers and mothers with children under five were evacuated from cities and urban areas in September 1939 in case of air raids. Parents were given instructions to pack a suitcase for their children which would be light enough for them to carry. Ask the children to think about what items parents may have packed in the cases. When they have an idea they should step into the circle, make the shape of the object and say what it is, for example, "I am a tooth brush." They can invite other pupils to help them make the shape if they need to. Encourage them to think of as many ideas as they can. Keep going until they run out of ideas or everybody has stepped into the circle.

Ask the students to re-form the circle and discuss whether there were any items which may not have existed in 1939. These items should be excluded from the next activity. Using masking tape, mark out a rectangle (approx 2m by 1.5m) on the floor to represent a suitcase. Ask the remaining objects to step back into their shapes in the circle – but not standing in the suitcase. Using the strategy of *Speaking Objects (p.76)* each object must justify why it should be packed in the suitcase. Select two children to represent the parents packing the case to question the objects. Once they have heard what all the objects have to say they should choose which ones should be packed - and these should stand in the "suitcase". Of course not every object will fit! Finally you can reveal the list of objects (see below)which the government instructed parents to pack.

 Tip:

An Evacuee's Suitcase

When evacuation is ordered your child should bring with him the following articles:

- *Gas Mask*
- *Spare stockings or socks*
- *Identity Card*
- *House shoes or plimsolls*
- *Ration Book*
- *Handkerchiefs*
- *Packet of food for the day*
- *Toothbrush*
- *Comb*
- *Change of underclothing*
- *Night Clothes*
- *Towel*
- *Warm coat or mackintosh*

At the Railway Station

This section uses audio from BBC School Radio and photographs of evacuees which can be sourced from books and websites.

Begin by playing **Audio 1**: *Children evacuated on 1 September 1939*

The recording provides background sounds and commentary of children waiting at Waterloo railway station to be evacuated. Discuss what is happening: the children are leaving their homes and parents to travel from urban areas to the countryside and may remain there for several years. The class will listen to you reading the story of a brother and sister who were evacuated at the ages of seven and ten.

Away From Home (Part One)

> It was a bright sunny morning as the crocodile of children wound its way towards Paddington Station. Among them was seven-year old Alice Taylor, clutching a large suitcase, a worn out teddy bear and wearing a small cardboard box strung around her neck. A long way ahead she could see Jack, her ten year old brother, in amongst the rest of his class. As they entered the station Alice could hardly believe her eyes. Hundreds of children thronged the platforms, carrying backpacks, pillowcases and even bulging coal sacks. Miss Meriwether, her form teacher, lined the class up in pairs.
>
> "Jack! Alice!" She turned round when she heard her name and saw a crowd of worried-looking women by the barrier waving their handkerchiefs. There at the back was her mother. Alice wanted to run back along the platform and hold on to her but Miss Meriwether gave her a stern look. The children had practised evacuation drill once already and been given strict instructions to stay together. Some of the class were crying but many of them looked quite excited about embarking on an adventure. The great railway engines were ready and waiting with plumes of smoke rising from their sooty funnels.
>
> "Maybe we're going to the seaside," whispered her friend Timothy Tucker, "Have you brought your bucket and spade?" Alice shrugged and checked that her name label was tied securely onto her coat. Before she knew it Jack was helping her scramble aboard with her heavy case. She held tightly to her teddy bear and the gas mask in its little box and looked back just as her mother shouted again, "Whatever you do, don't get separated from Jack! Write to me when you know where you're staying!" But Alice could hardly hear her through the sound of the excited voices, the thundering of the steam engine and the stationmaster's whistle as the train slowly left the station.

Show the class photographs of children being evacuated at railway stations and in train carriages (displaying a range of emotions). Ask the students to describe the different feelings being shown by the evacuees. Looking at the pictures, are there some things they would like to know more about? Beginning their sentences with "I wonder...", what questions can they ask? For example, "I wonder what's in that box," or "I wonder who the little girl is waving to." There is no need to answer these questions.

Divide the children into groups of four or five. Explain that you would like them to devise their own photograph of evacuees at the station by creating *tableaux* (p.67). Remind them to think about the emotions of each character and to show facial expressions as well as body posture. Give them a couple of minutes to discuss and work out their ideas. When the groups show their work you can use "I wonder..." as a way of drawing out what pupils think may be going on. You can use *spotlight (p.122)* to organise this and *thought tracking (p.31)* to allow individual characters to speak their thoughts and feelings aloud.

Rumours *(p.39)*

This story-making activity involves the whole class working together. Give the following instructions: "Imagine you are evacuees waiting for the train. Find a space and make a still image to show who you are and what you are doing. At the moment you know very little about what is happening today. What questions might you have in your mind? When I clap my hands you can begin to move around in character and whisper messages to the other chldren. You could ask questions or tell them some ideas about what you think is going to happen. If you hear something interesting you can pass it on to other people. Off you go."

After a couple of minutes call the children together and ask them to share what they heard and what they think might happen to the evacuees.

Role on the Wall *(p.34)*

Children can work in pairs or groups to draw a picture of an evacuee and add thought bubbles around the drawing to describe thoughts and feelings.

Journey and Arrival

Away From Home (Part Two)

> The train chugged out of London past rows and rows of houses. Alice and Jack were squashed together with their luggage in a completely packed carriage. Many children had never been on a train before and had their noses glued to the windows. Nobody seemed to have any idea where they were going – not even Miss Meriwether. The view through the windows changed as they moved into the countryside.
>
> "What are those?" asked Timothy Tucker. "Sheep – I think," said someone else. Before they knew it the whole carriage had started singing 'Old MacDonald's Farm' followed by 'Ten Green Bottles'. After almost eight long hours the train pulled into a station which didn't seem to have a name. The exhausted children took their luggage and were driven in an open-topped truck to a large hall with a crowd of local people waiting inside.

The evacuees were given a mug of cocoa and a sandwich, then a billeting officer read out names from a list. One by one the men and women stepped forward and took some children with them. Eventually there were only about half a dozen left, including Jack and Alice. "Climb up here where they can see you," said one of the billeting officers and they clambered up onto a stage. A few women went along the line, carefully looking them up and down, checking them for head-lice and examining their teeth. "I'll take that one," said one of them and grabbed Jack by the shoulder. "We've got to stay together!" cried Alice. "I don't need any more girls, I've got three of my own," replied the grumpy looking lady. She pulled Jack's arm but he refused to let go of Alice and eventually the woman gave in and led the pair of them with their bags along the street.

The lady (who was called Mrs Morgan) took them down a winding lane until they reached a house with a wide gate. The whole place smelled strange. Then a dog barked loudly and they thought they could hear cows mooing. A big man stood by the door, next to three girls. "Come in," he said cheerily. "Not yet," said Mrs Morgan and she whispered to the girls. They ran inside and brought out a big bowl of cold water. Before they knew it Mrs Morgan was scrubbing Jack and Alice from head to foot. "Just in case," she said. Shivering and wrapped in towels, the children were shown a room in the attic with a bed to share. It wasn't long before Alice's eyes started to close and she and Jack were fast asleep.

Tableaux

The children will work in small groups for the next task. Explain that they should create three group photographs, showing their own story about a day in the life of evacuee children. The first should show the children during the train journey; the second will show them being picked out by a parent from the host family and the third will show them meeting the new family. The students will need five to ten minutes to complete the task. When they have worked out the three tableaux, tell them that they need to practice so that everybody remembers their positioning. A good way to do this is for the teacher to count, "one-two-three" while all the groups go through their images at the same time.

When everybody is ready, sit the class down and *spotlight* (p.122) each group in turn by asking them to show the three tableaux as you count. Encourage the rest of the class to observe each member of the group carefully, so that they can try to guess what character and emotions they are representing. Discuss how groups have made it clear what is happening through the use of facial expression, body posture and the use of different levels – low, medium and high.

You can use different strategies with each group to vary the presentations. *Open and close (p.120)* works well with a series of images. *Thought tracking (p.31)* can be used at any point – and bringing the scene alive through *improvisation (p.96)* can be used for selected images. Another effective technique is to ask a group to move in slow-motion from one tableau to the next as you play some atmospheric music to heighten the drama *(p.68)*.

Settling In

To set the scene, play **Audio 2**: *Evacuees from Manchester interviewed* in which the children staying in a small Lancashire milltown in 1939 give their views on life with their new families in the countryside.

Away From Home (Part Three)

> *Over the next few days Alice got to know the sisters a bit better. Hettie (eleven years old), Edwina (nine) and Dora (seven) showed her around the farm and taught her how to muck out the stables while Mr Morgan began Jack's training in looking after the cattle. Alice went to school with Timothy Tucker in a local barn where Miss Meriwether taught the children history and times tables in amongst the clucking chickens.*
>
> *Jack was kept out of school to help on the farm and at night he told Alice about the jobs he'd been doing. It felt like they were on a big adventure together. But as Alice lay there she started to cry. "We'll never see Mum and Dad again. We won't never go home," she said, tears rolling down her face. "Don't be silly," said Jack. "We'll probably be back in a couple of weeks. Here," he said, offering a bag of barley sugar, "Have one of these. Go on, it'll make you feel better."*

Hot seating (p.28) gives an opportunity for the children to explore a number of roles and for you to evaluate their understanding of the evacuees' situation. A pair of children can play Jack and Alice (or other evacuee children) with the rest of the class asking questions. Encourage students to ask questions to find out how the character feels and to build up a background for the character (if they are confident, this activity can be done in small groups). They may also like to play other characters, such as foster parents or children already living in the village. If you wish, they can prepare backgrounds for their characters by planning them in groups using *role on the wall (p.34)*.

To help the children reflect on this activity and to consolidate the learning so far, play the following two audio extracts, which supply background details about the host families and their expectations.

Audio 3: *A host child describes his experiences*
Audio 4: *Host families interviewed*

Away From Home (Part Four)

> *Alice helped on the farm with Jack when she came home from school
> and at the weekends. She learnt how to milk the cows, collect hens'
> eggs and bake bread. The Morgan family took her and Jack to church
> twice every Sunday and while she was sitting on the hard wooden
> pew, Alice sometimes thought her Mum and Dad didn't care any
> more. They received weekly letters and had once been sent a parcel
> containing books and sweets. Even so, Alice couldn't help but wonder
> why her parents never came to visit. Then one Saturday afternoon
> she was outside feeding the chickens while Jack was chopping some
> wood, when a charabanc chugged up the lane and stopped right in
> front of the farmhouse. They couldn't believe their eyes when Mrs
> Taylor – their mother – stepped down off the bus.*

You can follow up this extract by using *teacher in role* (p.20) to play
Mrs Taylor (regardless of whether you are male or female). Explain that
you are going to pretend to be the children's mother after she has visited
Jack and Alice and that she wants to speak to the other evacuees in the
village. The pupils will take on those roles. You may wish to use an item of
costume or a prop to denote when you begin playing the role – or simply
turn your back on the class for a moment before you assume the character.

To help the students get into role you can begin by asking them how they
are finding their new lives in the village and whether they know how
Jack and Alice are settling in. You can describe how pleased you are to be
staying at Mrs Morgan's house for the weekend and how different it is to
your own. If they have already practiced being evacuees using hot-seating
then they will have a lot to say. This is also an opportunity to introduce
any information you wish, such as rationing, the "phoney war" and news
about the German invasions.

It is likely that some "evacuees" will express how much they are missing
their parents. You can suggest the idea that you would like to organise
another charabanc to bring more parents to visit their children. This can
lead on to *writing in role* (p.4) with the children writing letters to their
parents, describing their new home and asking them to visit. You can add
some urgency by explaining that Mrs Taylor would like to take these back
with her to London. Some parents did manage to organise such visits, but
it wasn't easy as the government tried to dissuade people from travelling.

The Letter

Away From Home (Part Five)

> *Three weeks later Mrs Taylor returned to the village with a whole coach load of Mums and Dads. The evacuee children were delighted and began looking forward to the visits once a month. After the second visit, Hettie asked, "Why don't you go home with your Mum? They're not even bombing London. It's just a phoney war!" Jack and Alice didn't know what to say at first, then Jack replied, "We can't go home. They won't let us. The Germans might bomb!" Later on he told Alice to ignore it. "Mr and Mrs Morgan are being paid to look after us and anyway we help on the farm," he said. Hettie and her sisters seemed to become even more unfriendly and then one cold February morning Alice found a letter in the dustbin with her name at the top. She opened up the crumpled paper and read:*

> *January 10th 1940*

> *Dear Jack and Alice,*

> *I hope you are both recovered from your chicken-pox. I have sent you some treats that I hope you enjoy. Dad has been called up for the army and will be leaving soon. I'm glad you are not in London any more as the Germans may soon bomb us. We have been told we may have to sleep in the tube stations.*

> *We won't be able to come in the charabancs for a while. I am knitting you each a new scarf and hope I can visit you again when things get easier.*

> *God bless and all my love,*

> *Mum.*

> *P.S. I have sent some extra money to Mrs Morgan as she says the money she gets from the government isn't enough.*

Give out photocopies of a handwritten version of Mum's letter for small groups to read. When they have finished reading, explain that you would like each group to devise a short improvised scene showing what Alice and Jack might decide to do. They can choose to have any characters they like in their scene and may use the letter as a prop. The discussion and rehearsal of these scenes provide an opportunity for the children to draw on the knowledge and understanding they have gained throughout this unit. When the groups perform the scenes it is likely that they will show a variety of decisions that Alice and Jack could make, such as writing to their mother, talking to Miss Meriwether or even running away.

Conscience alley (p.87) can be used to explore these choices. Ask the class to form two lines facing each other. One person (the teacher or a child) takes the role of Alice and walks between the lines as each member of the class speaks their advice. Whoever is playing Alice can hold the letter and slowly walk between the lines as she listens to the advice. You can, for example, ask one side to try and persuade Alice to run away and the other to give her reasons to stay and respond to the letter in a different way. When Alice reaches the end of the alley she should announce her decision. This can also be done with two children walking down the alley together as Alice and Jack.

Resources:

★   *WW2 People's War* is an online archive of wartime memories contributed by members of the public and gathered by the BBC. It contains many true accounts by evacuees. The archive can be found at: www.bbc. co.uk/ww2peopleswar.

★   The audio files can be found at:
   www.bbc.co.uk/schoolradio/subjects/history/ww2clips.

★   These links and others can be found in one place at:
   www.LearningThroughDrama.com.

Glossary

Bags and Boxes *59*	Objects in a bag or box are used to support storytelling and to stimulate creative and narrative skills.
Conscience Alley *87*	A character walks down an alleyway formed by members of the class as they use persuasive arguments to help make a decision.
Essence Machines *82*	Students work together to make repeating sounds and movements based on a theme – producing a machine-like effect.
Flashbacks / Flash Forwards *104*	Participants improvise events that take place before or after a specific moment in time enabling the exploration of characters' motivations and the consequences of their actions.
Forum Theatre *98*	Members of the audience are invited to take part in an improvised drama to explore alternative approaches to a problem.
Guided Tour *54*	An orally described journey by the teacher or children or a sensory tour where one student leads a blindfolded partner while describing the imaginary surroundings.
Hot Seating *29*	The student or teacher answers questions in role about the background, behaviour and motivation of a character.
Improvisation *95*	Improvisation is the spontaneous performance of a scene or story.
Living Newspaper *110*	A thematic approach for linking and presenting a montage of students' work using a range of drama strategies.
Mantle of the Expert *25*	The creation of a fictional world where students assume the roles of experts in a designated field.
Marking the Moment *108*	A drama technique used to highlight a key moment in an improvisation.

(Page references in italics)

Meetings *37*	An improvised gathering held in role to discuss views about a problem and how it can be resolved.
Mime *79*	The use of physical movement to imaginatively explore activities in role or to communicate stories and characters.
Narration (students) *51*	Storytelling used by the students to structure their performance.
Narration (teacher) *49*	Storytelling used by the teacher to shape the drama.
Object Theatre *118*	Everyday objects are brought to life through simple puppetry.
One Word At A Time *57*	Students tell a story by taking it in turns to speak one word at a time.
Open and Close *120*	A technique for telling a story through a series of still images, where the audience open and close their eyes to keep each image clear and separate in their minds.
Ritual *106*	A specially devised sequence of words and movements to mark an important point in a drama.
Role On The Wall *34*	A collaborative way of generating information and ideas about a character through written contributions to a drawing.
Role Play *17*	The student takes on the role of a character to explore an alternative point of view.
Rumours *39*	Improvised comments are passed amongst students to generate and spread ideas about characters or situations.
Sculpting *71*	Students model each other into shapes to represent characters or objects.
Soundscape *101*	Students create the atmosphere of a scene or environment by making appropriate sounds with their bodies and voices. Musical instruments, physical objects and recordings can also be used.

(Page references in italics)

Speaking Objects *76*	Students make the shapes of objects and speak aloud what they might be observing and feeling.
Spotlight *122*	Spotlighting is a technique for enabling small groups to share their improvisational work.
Still Images and Freeze-Frames *63*	Still images or freeze-frames are physical shapes created by individuals or groups using their bodies.
Storytelling *45*	One of the simplest and perhaps most compelling forms of dramatic and imaginative activity.
Tableaux *67*	Students make still images with their bodies to represent a scene.
Teacher in Role *20*	The teacher (or other adult) assumes the role of a character to guide and develop students' learning.
Telephone Conversations *42*	Pupils speak in role as though having a conversation on the telephone.
Ten Second Objects *73*	Groups of students use their bodies to quickly make an overall physical shape.
Thought Tracking *31*	Students speak aloud the thoughtsof their character in a still image.
Visualisation *52*	Students close their eyes to visualise images, stories and places while listening to narration, storytelling, poetry or music.
Where Do You Stand? *90*	Students express their views by choosing where to stand on a line representing a continuum of opinion.
Whole Class Drama *2*	The whole class becomes involved in an extended drama focussing on learning and enquiry rather than performance.
Whoosh! *114*	A quick and interactive way of teaching a story plot to children of all ages – in a way they will remember!

(Page references in italics)

References

Andreae (2001). *Giraffes Can't Dance*. Orchard Books.

Baldwin, P. (2008). *The Primary Drama Handbook*. Sage Publications.

Boal, A. (1995). *The Rainbow of Desire*. Routledge.

Boal, A. (1979). *Theatre of the Oppressed*. Pluto Press.

Bolton, G. (1979). *Towards a Theory of Drama in Education*. Longman.

Burrell, J. (2007). Mantle of the Expert – The Sea Company. [Online]. (URL http://www.moeplanning.co.uk/wp-content/uploads/2008/04/nut-mag-article-on-moe.pdf). *NUT Magazine*, September 2007. (Accessed 15 June 2011).

Corbett, P. (2009). *Jumpstart! Storymaking*. David Fulton.

Donaldson, J. (1999) *The Gruffalo*. Macmillan.

Farmer, D. (2007). *101 Drama Games and Activities*. Lulu Press.

Gilbert, I. (2007). *The Little Book of Thunks*. Crown House Publishing.

Goodwin, J. (2006). *Using Drama to Support Literacy*. Paul Chapman.

Hoffman, M. (2007). *Amazing Grace*. Frances Lincoln Children's Books.

Hopkins, B. (2004). *Just Schools*. Jessica Kingsley.

Hughes, E. (1968). *The Iron Man*. Faber and Faber.

Johnson, K. (1979). *Impro: Improvisation and the Theatre*. Faber and Faber.

Lobman, C and Lundquist, M. (2007). *Unscripted Learning*. Teachers College Press.

Munsch, R. (1980). *The Paper Bag Princess*. Annick Press.

Paley, V. (1990). *The Boy Who Would be a Helicopter*. Harvard University Press.

Peter, M. (1996). Developing Drama From Story. *In:* Kemp A., ed. *Drama Education and Special Needs*. Stanley Thornes Ltd.

Neelands, J and Goode, A. (1990). *Structuring Drama Work*. Cambridge University Press.

Rosen, M. (1993). *We're Going on a Bear Hunt*. Walker Books.

Rowling, J. K. (2001) *Harry Potter and the Philosopher's Stone*. Bloomsbury Publishing.

Royal Shakespeare Company (2010). *The RSC Shakespeare Toolkit for Teachers*. Methuen Drama.

Simon, F. and Ross, T. (1998) *Horrid Henry*. Orion Children's Books.

Thorsborne, M and Vinegrad, D (2009). *Restorative Justice Pocketbook*. Alresford: Teachers' Pocketbooks

Trivizas, E. (2003). *The Three Little Wolves and the Big Bad Pig*. Egmont Books.

Velthuijs, M. (1994) *Frog in Winter*. Andersen Press.

Waddell, M. (1991). *Farmer Duck*. Walker Books.

Wagner, B. J. (1976). *Dorothy Heathcote, Drama as a Learning Medium*. Hutchinson.

Winston, J and Tandy, M. (1998). *Beginning Drama 4-11*. David Fulton.

Further Resources

Audacity *Sound editing software* www.audacity.sourceforge.net
Comic Life *Comic making software* www.plasq.com
MakeBelieve Arts *The Helicopter Technique* www.makebelievearts.co.uk
Mantle of the Expert www.mantleoftheexpert.com
Restorative Justice www.restorativejustice.org.uk, www.transformingconflict.org
Shakespeare: www.shakespeare-literature.com, www.rsc.org.uk

Index

Website of the Book

There is a web site for this book at **www.LearningThroughDrama.com** where you can submit suggestions and access additional resources such as current links, worksheets and article updates. If you have any comments or ideas to add, please visit the site where you can help contribute to the next edition!

The author's website at **www.DramaResource.com** contains ever-growing resources for teaching drama – including games, strategies, lesson plans and one-day courses where you are invited to experience and explore these ideas with like-minded people. You can also sign up to the free *Drama Resource Newsletter* bringing monthly news and resources to your desktop.

Notes

Alphabetical List of Drama Strategies

(With page numbers for easy reference.)

Notes

Notes

Printed in Poland
by Amazon Fulfillment
Poland Sp. z o.o., Wrocław

50378613R00101